"MINECRAFT IS INDEED AN UNLIKELY TALE. THAT'S WHAT MAKES IT SO GREAT, AND THAT'S WHY THIS LITTLE BOOK WILL MAKE A TERRIFIC HOLIDAY GIFT FOR THE GAMER IN YOUR LIFE."
—ANDREW LEONARD, SALON

"YOU LEARN ABOUT THE MAN BEHIND THE GAME. HIS CHILDHOOD, HIS FAMILY, THE GROWTH OF HIS COMPANY, AND THE LIVES OF THE PEOPLE WHO WORK THERE. IT DOESN'T JUST GIVE YOU THE BIG, ENORMOUS, GLAMOUR-FILLED CUT SCENES THAT YOU READ ABOUT ON THE INTERNET. THIS BOOK GIVES YOU THE PIXELS, THE DETAILS."
—BOOK RIOT

"SUSPENSEFUL, GROUNDED, AND START-LINGLY RELATABLE. A PERFECT GIFT FOR MINECRAFT PLAYERS, PARENTS OF YOUNGER PLAYERS, OR ANYONE INTERESTED IN INDIE GAMES."
—GAMESKINNY

"THIS BOOK EXPLORES THE MAN BEHIND THE GAME TO A DEPTH THAT YOU WON'T, AND THAT YOU CAN'T, FIND ANYWHERE ELSE."
—SETHBLING, MINECRAFT VIDEO MAKER

MINECRAFT

SECOND EDITION

MINECRAFT

**THE UNLIKELY TALE OF MARKUS "NOTCH" PERSSON
AND THE GAME THAT CHANGED EVERYTHING**

DANIEL GOLDBERG

&

LINUS LARSSON

TRANSLATION BY
JENNIFER HAWKINS

NEW YORK ■ OAKLAND

SEVEN STORIES PRESS
140 WATTS STREET
NEW YORK, NY 10013
WWW.SEVENSTORIES.COM

COLLEGE PROFESSORS MAY ORDER EXAMINATION COPIES OF SEVEN
STORIES PRESS TITLES FOR FREE. TO ORDER, VISIT HTTP://WWW.
SEVENSTORIES.COM/TEXTBOOK OR SEND A FAX ON SCHOOL LETTERHEAD
TO (212) 226-1411.

BOOK DESIGN BY JANET BRUESSELBACH

FRONTIS: MARKUS PERSSON. PHOTO BY KRISTINA SAHLÉN

LIBRARY OF CONGRESS CATALOGING-IN-PUBLICATION DATA
GOLDBERG, DANIEL, 1982-
[MINECRAFT. ENGLISH]
MINECRAFT : THE UNLIKELY TALE OF MARKUS "NOTCH" PERSSON AND
THE GAME THAT CHANGED EVERYTHING / DANIEL GOLDBERG AND LINUS
LARSSON ; TRANSLATION BY JENNIFER HAWKINS.
PAGES CM.
ORIGINALLY PUBLISHED IN SWEDISH AS "MINECRAFT: BLOCK, PIXLAR
OCH ATT GORA SIG EN HACKA."
ISBN 978-1-60980-537-1
ISBN 978-1-60980-575-3 (2ND ED)
1. PERSSON, MARKUS, 1979- 2. MINECRAFT (GAME) 3. COMPUTER
PROGRAMMERS 4. COMPUTER GAMES 5. COMPUTER GAMES--DESIGN
I. LARSSON, LINUS, AUTHOR. II. TITLE.
GV1463.G65 2013
794.8--DC23
2013016343

PRINTED IN THE UNITED STATES

9 8 7 6 5 4 3 2 1

PART ONE

CHAPTER 1

THREE, TWO, ONE . . .

IT'S NOVEMBER 18, 2011. An old man in a faded gray sweater looks up from his slot machine. A long and steady stream of children, teens, and grown-ups flows through the casino. Their outfits are odd, even for this place. In Las Vegas, you can count on seeing pretty much anything: Elvis impersonators lined up on the sidewalks, gigantic fake-gold lions, drunken weekend revelers, and fountains shooting water hundreds of yards into the air synchronized to the tune of the national anthem.

The people streaming through the casino at the Hotel

Mandalay Bay are wearing cardboard boxes on their heads. Some are in full cardboard-box bodysuits with armholes that look uncomfortable and make their elbows stick straight out, like cubist comic-strip characters with the posture of bodybuilders. The cardboard suits they've squeezed into are painted in large colorful squares, some green, some black. Others are light blue, brown, and pink. The man at the slot machines, clueless, returns to his game, his cigarette, and his morning cocktail.

The cardboard-box people aren't there to win money. They continue toward the convention facilities that are next to the casino, where in a few minutes they will be cheering as they watch a thirty-two-year-old Swede pull a lever and release the finished version of their favorite game.

Minecraft. A computer game as incomprehensible to the uninitiated as it is wildly adored by tens of millions of people. Those who've traveled here are among the game's most devoted fans. Not only have they paid airfare but also, before embarking for Las Vegas, they cut and glued their suits, modeled on the game's primitive block graphics and shapes.

And there are thousands of them, representing a total of twenty-three countries. The youngest is four years old and the oldest is seventy-seven. Of the many parents, some have made the trip just for their kids and are now observing in awe a world their offspring adore but that is alien to them. Others are just as passionate as their children.

"We play together constantly," says a dad with green-tinted hair, wearing a suit sprayed green, his face covered with black bars as he poses for pictures with his identically decked-out son.

A few minutes later. The convention hall where we're seated is the largest at the Mandalay Bay. It's completely packed and the lights are off. All eyes turn toward the stage and Lydia Winters, who—impossible not to recognize with her short, shocking pink hair—is firing up the audience.

"This weekend is going to be awesome!"

Giant screens are mounted on both sides of the stage so that those sitting farther back can see what's happening. They all show Lydia's happy, glowing, almost cartoon-character-like smile.

"So many people's . . . *lives* have been changed by this game!"

Next to the stage, just to the left, the weekend's big star is waiting for the signal to step up into the spotlight: Markus Persson, dressed in jeans, well-worn sneakers, and a black polo that's a bit tight around the middle. As always, he's wearing a black fedora. Markus doesn't know what to do with his hands while he waits. He pulls absentmindedly at the hem of his shirt before his hands land in his jeans pockets, thumbs out.

There is an ocean of five thousand people seated before him—if *seated* is the right word, because many of them stand up as the first of Markus's colleagues arrive onstage. Lydia Winters calls them up and one by one they trudge onstage, shyly wave a little at the audience, and line up beside her. Jens Bergensten—the programmer, tall, lanky, his red ponytail hanging down his back. Carl Manneh—the CEO, who is perfectly okay with Lydia keeping the microphone. Jakob Porser—Markus's old friend and the cofounder of his company. The graphics guy, Junkboy—no, his real name is never given in public—who leaps onstage wearing a cardboard box on his head and making victory signs for the audience. They're all Swedish men, all in their late twenties and early thirties, and they all work at Mojang, the company that produces *Minecraft*. Most days they sit and work at their computers in a shabby apartment on Åsögatan, in Stockholm. But this is no ordinary day.

This is the moment when the final version of *Minecraft* will be released to the public. Which means that until today, the five thousand people in the audience—and several million others around the world—have been playing an unfinished game. A kind of prototype, which has earned Markus close to $70 million and created one of the world's most admired companies.

This is MineCon, the first convention dedicated entirely to *Minecraft*. The event began as a random idea at the Mojang headquarters on Södermalm, in southern Stockholm. Markus Persson asked on his blog if anyone would pay ninety dollars to go to a *Minecraft* convention in Las Vegas. Within a few weeks more than 43,000 people said they would, and the Mandalay Bay was booked. The hotel is a forty-four-story monumental monstrosity built entirely of gold-tinted glass. In its twenty-two restaurants, smoke-filled poker dens, and meandering indoor malls, you can easily spend several days without leaving the hotel—exactly as intended. As a rule, casinos in Las Vegas have no windows or clocks, so that gamblers will continue to feed money into the machines throughout the night. The desert gambling mecca is no place for people with regular circadian rhythms.

The coming days will be an unparalleled spectacle, bizarre for those unfamiliar with gaming conventions in general and especially so for those who don't know *Minecraft* in particular. People will line up for hours to get Markus's autograph. A costume contest will nearly degenerate into a riot. Two British men, known by millions of fans from their YouTube channel, will be greeted like celebrities when they play videos on the stage, showing functioning electronic equipment built entirely within *Minecraft*.

It's not that surprising. *Minecraft* had grown into an unprecedented success story well before MineCon. Sixteen million players had downloaded the game; more than four million of them had paid for it. *Minecraft* had been praised by pretty much every gaming magazine and website in the world. And after all, it's a game so engrossing that thousands of its most faithful fans have traveled to Las Vegas to celebrate that it is finally finished.

We have come here to understand why. We want to ask the costumed men and women what it is about *Minecraft* that makes them love it more than any other game. And not least of all, we want to know why Markus's strange creation has earned him such enormous sums of money. For it was, of course, the money that made us take note of Markus Persson in the first place. In late 2010, the unassuming programmer began to pop up in interviews, describing how he'd struck gold with his remarkable game. He always displayed a modest, almost surprised demeanor in the face of his success. He didn't seem to have any idea what to do with his millions.

It looked like an improbable business success, a story of a quick breakthrough and of sudden riches, a shining example of how the Internet can shake the foundations of an industry and create empires within months. But the closer we looked, the more difficult it was to fit *Minecraft* into the usual frameworks. There was no successful marketing strategy to point to, no business plan that held the secrets to success. There was just one guy with his own, slightly odd idea of what the gaming world needed. The story that emerged had very little to do with polished businessmen and fast deals. Instead, we found an idea rooted in Markus's childhood, one that could only blossom outside the established framework of the gaming industry.

Actually, it's only now, seated a few yards from the stage, that we fully understand what a star Markus is. Lydia Winters continues her exuberant introduction as we scan the crowd. There's a woman crying in the row in front of us, which is reserved for special guests. Her cheeks are pierced and she has henna-colored hair and red scars in intricate patterns on her arms. There is also a short girl holding a camera, beaming with pride. Right beside her, there's an older Swedish gentleman and a lady with shoulder-length, pure-white hair.

"This all started because of one person," says Lydia. If anyone had entered the hall at that moment without knowing what was going on, that person would have guessed she was talking about a prophet. The room erupts in cheers.

"I think we need to do better than that. I think we need to *chant* to get him up onstage."

The whole audience responds to Lydia's suggestion. The roar is deafening. "Notch! Notch! Notch!" Few people in the room know him as Markus.

Down beside the stage, thoughts race through Markus's head. What should he say? He has always hated speaking in public. On Twitter, he writes for half a million people,

2

but this is different. Onstage, there's no backing up and no erasing what he's said. It's all live, going out directly, both to people on-site and to those following the event online.

Forty minutes earlier, he had asked for a drink to calm his nerves. Someone put a glass of vodka in his hand. Now he's standing there trying to figure out if he's drunk or not. Shouldn't he be more nervous? There was something about the stairs too—he shouldn't look out at the audience when he walks up onstage, someone had said. He might trip.

Markus carefully climbs onto the stage. He looks self-conscious, but breaks out in a timid smile when he holds up his hand to wave to the audience. The spotlights seem to blind him completely. Lydia, whose neon-colored hair is accentuated by her all-black clothing, tries to get a few words out of Markus. He says something about "grateful" and "cool."

"I love you, Notch!" someone from the audience cries. Markus squirms.

The stage decor consists of paper models and figures resembling those in the game. One life-size human figure looks exactly like Steve, the *Minecraft* protagonist. There's a green monster, some boxes, and a column of blocks sporting a lever. The lever's not actually connected to anything, but the energy level in the room rises when Markus approaches it.

"Are you ready for the official release of *Minecraaaaaaaaft?*" Lydia roars.

The audience roars back. A techno beat begins to pump. But Markus hesitates, grips the lever, lets it go again. Camera flashes and the noise level in the hall begin to approach the limits of human tolerance. Finally, Markus gives the lever a push. Fireworks explode and confetti shoots out over the sea of faces. The music gets even louder and the programmers onstage break out dancing, as *Minecraft 1.0* is finally released to the world. Markus, off to the side, just nods his head to the beat. At that moment, a technician behind the stage tells us, four thousand people are logging in to play *Minecraft*. Four thousand per second, that is.

Jakob, the old friend from an earlier time, dances up to Markus and receives a hug that lifts him off the floor.

The Mojang team on stage at MineCon 2011 in Las Vegas. Photo courtesy of Mojang.

CHAPTER 2

FOR BEGINNERS

FIRST-TIME *MINECRAFT* **PLAYERS** are usually struck by how simplistic it all looks. Ugly, some would say. But those who know their gaming history will feel instantly at home.

If you look closely enough at a computer or TV screen, you'll see the dots that make up the image. These points—pixels—are the atoms of computer graphics, the smallest indivisible units. Hardware and software developers harbor a kind of love-hate relationship with the pixel. When Apple released the iPhone 4, Steve Jobs made a big deal about the screen, which he called Retina

Display. The idea was that each dot on the screen was so small, the resolution so high, that it would be impossible for the human eye to distinguish between separate pixels, and the last remnants of "computer feel" would vanish. Apple had won the war on the pixel.

In other circles, the pixel is lovingly embraced. Extracting maximum meaning from the fewest pixels is an art form as old as computer gaming. The classic arcade game *Pong* is just a square dot that bounces between two flat surfaces, but to the player, it's obviously a game of tennis. In the first version of *Super Mario Bros.*, Mario was only sixteen pixels tall and twelve pixels wide. However, there is no doubt that the little cluster of colored pixels represents a mustachioed Italian plumber wearing a red cap and suspenders.

Today, the limitations of hardware are no longer a problem, but the logic of the pixel continues to affect the gaming world. Place four pixels in a square and you get a block; pile the blocks on top of each other and you get a tower; arrange them diagonally and you have stairs. The worlds in the *Super Mario* games are still built of blocks, placed side by side to create platforms to stand on, or on top of each other to create walls. Certain blocks can be destroyed, but new blocks can't be created. And the whole point of *Tetris* is to eliminate blocks by arranging them in rows as they fall slowly down the screen.

The breakthroughs in 3-D graphics did not mean that

the blocks disappeared. Instead, the two-dimensional squares became boxes. Block puzzles, in which objects are moved around to fit into predetermined patterns, popped up in all imaginable kinds of games, kind of like homages to the early days of video games when everything was blocky, charmingly clumsy, and square out of pure necessity. But boxes and blocks also lend themselves to building games—we have all played with blocks as kids, piled them on top of each other, toppled them, and arranged them side by side to make patterns.

Minecraft embraces the pixel. The ground, trees, mountains—and everything else in Markus's creation—are built of identically sized, one cubic meter blocks. Colors vary, depending on what the different blocks represent. Grass blocks are green on the top and brown farther down; mountain blocks are gray; tree trunks are brown (except for birches, which are black-and-white, as in reality).

But then, this is no paltry little toy world that the player finds himself or herself in, after having seemingly fallen out of the sky for no apparent reason. Huge green spaces stretch out in one direction, a gigantic ocean in the other, and in the distance—how far you can see depends on how powerful your computer is—you glimpse a cloud-covered mountaintop. Amid the trees and quadrangular pigs, cows, and sheep scampering idly around is the player, represented by the blocky avatar, Steve. There is no given direction to move in, no obstacles to climb over nor enemies to defeat. The player receives no instructions whatsoever. Exactly how the world looks changes every time, as the scenery is randomly generated before each new game. The code that generates these worlds is, to say the least, complicated, for while chance determines the appearance of the world, there always has to be natural transitions between mountains, steppes, water, and caves. Markus is the only one who really understands how it all works.

This is where some people stop playing *Minecraft*. Others, however, begin to dig, because every single block in the *Minecraft* world can be hacked free from the environment and rearranged in a new formation of the player's design. Put enough blocks in the right places and you have a simple shelter; a few more will turn that shelter into a house—or a barn, a fort, a spaceship, or an exact replica of the Reichstag building in Berlin. But we're getting ahead of ourselves. Most people are content with building a simple shelter at first, and in fact, they have to. Because after ten minutes the sun goes down and *Minecraft* day transitions into *Minecraft* night, and at night monsters come out. By that time, it's important to have used enough dirt clods or stones to build something that they can't get into. A player's first shelter isn't usually very impressive, but it only has to be good enough to protect you from the skeletons, spiders, and zombies that wander the dark. Not to mention the most infamous *Minecraft* monster of all: the Creeper.

The Creeper is a creature known by its green blockish shape and characteristic black pixel face. When a Creeper approaches the player, it starts to hiss like a lit fuse on a stick of cartoon dynamite; then it grows, blinks white, and finally explodes, taking the player down with it. In October 2010, Markus Persson announced on Twitter that the Creeper is "crunchy, like dry leaves," and even though such qualities cannot possibly emerge in the low-resolution game world, this description has since become an uncontested part of *Minecraft* lore.

The story of how the Creeper came to be is emblematic of how *Minecraft* was developed. Markus has apologized for the game's simple (though according to many, ingenious) graphics by saying that he just wasn't able to create anything more sophisticated at the time, but the Creeper really takes limited invention to a new level— it was made by mistake. While trying to design a pig, Markus mixed up the variables for height and length and the result was a standing form with four smaller blocks for legs. With a little greenish tint and a ghostly face, the monster was complete. Today, the Creeper has been immortalized on T-shirts, in the *Minecraft* logo, on decals, and with innumerable homemade costumes.

Minecraft does offer the player a lot of conventional

gaming recreation. You can, for example, build portals to parallel dimensions, explore abandoned ruins, fight with a sword, and face dragons in life-and-death battles. But the players who focus on these things are missing the point: *Minecraft* is about building. After building the first shelter, to protect from the monsters of the night, a deeply rooted human need sets in—the need to build new things, to construct something more advanced, or to just create nicer surroundings. It's even possible to play in a mode where monsters don't come out and attack at night and where the supply of resources—sorry, blocks—is infinite. It's called Creative Mode.

When those who enter Markus Persson's world do so without interfering enemies and can invest all their energy in building, their creativity takes off. Placing one block upon another, over and over, can yield the most spectacular creations. The largest ones are created by several players working together for weeks, maybe even months. As listing all of the impressive feats of construction would demand a book of its own, we'll settle for a small sample:

THE EIFFEL TOWER. Actually, many versions of Paris's iconic landmark have been constructed. Some builders, who kept the height down to around 30 meters, have publicly apologized for their lack of ambition and promised that future buildings will be more true to life.

THE STARSHIP *ENTERPRISE,* the giant spaceship from *Star Trek,* re-created block by block in as elaborate detail as the one-meter cubes will allow.

NOTRE DAME CATHEDRAL, in full scale. The originator proudly declared that the cathedral was created in Survival Mode, with monsters lurking at night.

AN ELECTRIC ORGAN, fully functional and with several voices, playing Johann Sebastian Bach's *Air on the G String*.

THE TAJ MAHAL, in several versions.

THE PLANET EARTH. Not full scale, but big enough to astound anyone who appreciates how time-consuming it is to build anything out of cubic meter blocks.

And this is still just the beginning. Of the many building materials to be found in the world of *Minecraft*, there is one known for its conductivity: redstone. These blocks are best regarded as a basic programming language, and can be used to build electronic equipment. A player piano, a slot machine, or a fully functional calculator, for example. Or why not a version of *Minecraft*, played on a computer built inside of *Minecraft*? Perhaps this is why *Minecraft* is so unique: the most devoted players choose to exclude everything in it that is reminiscent of more conventional games; they don't care about killing enemies, exploring caves, or slaying dragons. They only want to build. Bigger, more beautiful, more complicated, and more impressive.

That doesn't make *Minecraft* less of a game, just a very different game. There's nothing here that can be called a climax; there's not even any real rules or challenges to get past. *Minecraft* can be thought of as an enormous sandbox where imagination reigns. The purpose of the game becomes whatever the player decides to create: an even more detailed Taj Mahal, a copy of the Royal Palace in Stockholm, an electric organ with more voices than anyone else has succeeded in putting together, or maybe just a little red cabin with white trim. The game can be made just as simple—or complex—as the player wishes it to be.

So, if *Minecraft* isn't a game in the usual sense of the word, what is it? Maybe it can be thought of as LEGO pieces on steroids; LEGO pieces that you can build larger and more advanced buildings with. LEGO pieces are, of course, sold in kits, intended to be put together according to predetermined designs. But it usually doesn't take long before all the pieces are mixed up. True creativity isn't unleashed until they're lying all over the place.

In *Minecraft*, no particular block has any predetermined place in a construction. A black block can be part of the nose of a giant Mickey Mouse statue, included in a ballroom floor, or become part of the foundation of the Great Pyramid of Giza. Just like LEGO pieces, *Minecraft* gives the player infinite freedom to create, while the potential is strictly set by the characteristics of the raw materials. A block is always a block, but enough blocks can become anything the player can imagine.

When Markus Persson pulled the lever on the stage in Las Vegas, *Minecraft* was already a world sensation. In the spring of 2012, his game had more than three times as many players as the population of Sweden. Just a few years before that it was far from obvious that he would become known outside the small circle of initiates who understand and appreciate obscure independent games.

Many games have been sold in larger numbers than *Minecraft*—most notably, those released by the large game companies, with their thousands of employees and billions of dollars in annual turnover. Those games are pressed onto the market with worldwide advertising campaigns to shore them up. They're always sold in boxes on retail-store shelves, like any product, and cost many weeks' allowances. The themes are, of course, just as magnificent as they are deadly serious: war with automatic weapons, battlefields in fantasy environments, and interactive space sagas for science fiction buffs. These games are polished and photorealistic down to the last detail, and have well-paid Hollywood actors doing the voiceovers. Games that sell will have sequels. Games that do well after that may be turned into franchises. And so on, until every possible dollar has been sucked from the original concept.

And then we have *Minecraft*: a game developed by one single person in Stockholm, with graphics so pixely simple that it makes you think of the 1980s. An idea that, if it had been proposed to an investor, would have been immediately sent to the circular file, but that, against all odds, became perhaps the most iconic and talked-about game since *Tetris*. To understand how it all began, we need to go to Sweden, to an apartment in a suburb of Stockholm, and to a time when nothing looked like it was moving in the right direction for Markus Persson.

CHAPTER 3

"DO YOU WANT ME TO FEEL SORRY FOR YOU OR SOMETHING?"

THE SAME SCENARIO greeted Ritva Persson each evening. She'd finished her nursing shift, gone home to the apartment, and walked in the door to the sound of Markus's keyboard clattering in his room. High school was over, but her son showed no signs of moving out. He showed very few signs of anything at all, in fact. Often, when Ritva returned from a full day at work, Markus had been sitting at his computer the whole time. His hours spent in front of the screen were divided between playing simple, nerdy games and programming his own, just-as-simple, just-as-nerdy games. Even though his creations were nothing extraordinary, Markus liked watching them materialize before his eyes. When he was absorbed in his code, nothing else around him mattered. It would be a gross exaggeration to say that Markus had a life plan, but if there was one thing he was sure of, it was that he liked creating games. His dream was to make a career of it, and ideally, those games would be his own.

That Markus was shy was no news. Ever since his family had moved from the small town of Edsbyn to the city of Stockholm, he had preferred to keep to himself. Life in the small town had been different. His family moved there when Markus was a newborn, bought some land, and then built a house while Ritva was pregnant with Markus's little sister, Anna. Markus's father, Birger, got a job at the national railroad company, and Ritva commuted to the hospital in Bollnäs. Even then Markus loved building with LEGO pieces, but in Edsbyn he also played with the neighboring kids. He was kind of the tough guy in his little group, the one who came up with the pranks that the others went along with.

Markus remembers how he changed after the move to Stockholm. When he started at the Skogsängs School in Salem, he was put in a class with kids who had already had six months to get to know each other, and it took a while for Markus to fit in. He spent every day alone with his LEGO pieces, which he stored unsorted in an old school desk (the wooden kind, with a flip-up lid). Sometimes, he'd turn the pieces into spaceships and then dismantle them; other times he built a car—just to see if it would survive the trip down a small incline that Markus had chosen for exactly that purpose. If the car made it all the way down, it was branded a success and he would take it apart and use the pieces for something new. Every year as Christmas approached, more LEGO pieces were at the top of his list.

Markus's interest was diverted only when his father came home one day from work carrying a large box in his arms. Proudly, Birger opened it in front of the family and lifted out a Commodore 128, the more advanced sibling of the iconic gaming computer, Commodore 64. The family set up the machine in the parents' bedroom and it immediately became, as far as Markus was concerned, the focal point of the home. Some simple games came along with the new computer, but even more interesting to seven-year-old Markus was the programming instructions, which he read through with Birger guiding him. They sat together in front of the monitor every evening, and it was his dad whom Markus called over to come see the end results of his early exercises in programming.

The computer opened up a new world to Markus. Just as building with LEGO pieces was more fun than playing with ready-made cars and spaceships, there was something special about entering code in the machine and getting it to perform. Markus's first original games were text adventures based on a cowboys-and-Indians theme. Perhaps the simplest form of game, a text adventure is more like an interactive novel where the player engages through text than what we've come to expect from computer games. For example, the player may be put in front of a house and must choose, by typing a command, between entering through the door, breaking the window, or turning around. Depending on which option he or she chooses, the story unfolds in different ways. The biggest flaw in Markus's creation was that he didn't know how to save the code, and so each time the computer was shut down, everything disappeared and the next day he would have to begin all over again. Maybe you need the tenacity of a seven-year-old to continue under such circumstances.

Whenever Markus wasn't doing his own programming, he was playing games. The classic puzzle game *Boulder Dash*, in which the player's mission is to dig around in caves, watch out for enemies, and collect valuable gemstones for points, was a favorite of his. He also played the action game *Saboteur*, and the role-playing game *The Bard's Tale* (the first game he bought with his own money). As they all were in those days, the games were simplistic creations with pixely graphics and squeaky, hissing digital sounds for music. Markus could sit for hours in front of the computer with his trusty plastic joystick in his grip and his cassette player spinning in the background.

Markus had no trouble with any of his classes. In fact, school was so easy that he started trying to stay home. It wasn't like he was cutting classes; Ritva remembers how he'd tell her he had a stomachache or some other vague symptom just serious enough for him to be able to stay home and slip into his parents' bedroom and to the computer.

When Ritva's days off from work coincided with Markus's "sick" days, she became worried by how engrossed Markus was in the computer. It was the 1980s, the debates about video violence raged on, and something as new as computers—in homes, no less!—was depicted as dangerous for your eyes and your child's development. *He should get out more*, she thought. *Play soccer, be with the other kids.* She wanted to see him come home with rosy cheeks, exhausted from an afternoon of fresh air, not sunk down in front of the computer like a sack of potatoes. She considered limiting his time at the computer, but soon realized it would be like trying to stop an avalanche with her bare hands.

Instead, she tried subterfuge. When Markus wasn't at home, she snuck into his room and put up posters of soccer players—no one remembers which—that Markus immediately tore down with a caustic comment that no one else should try to decide what he would have on his walls. Ritva even dragged Markus to the local soccer club. After he had stumbled around the field, missed the balls, and avoided scoring, the coach took Ritva aside. "Nothing will probably come of this," she remembers him saying. "He's not going to be a soccer player."

Ritva was successful, however, in getting both Markus and Anna to go to church. Though Markus seldom talks about growing up in a religious, evangelical family, his parents had actually met each other through the Pentecostal movement. Virtually every Sunday, the family took the commuter train into the city, got off at the T-Centralen subway station, and walked to the City Church in the center of the city. Markus mostly remembers the services as boring. But he did believe in God.

Eventually, Markus found a small group of friends at school who also had particular interests. One showed a great musical talent; another was, like Markus, more interested in technology and logical constructions. Everyone in his small circle got good grades and each had a single passion in life. They were, if we may use a tired expression, nerds. At some point in middle school, they added tabletop role-playing games to their list of activities, which got Markus to reveal a new side of his personality. In every other context he preferred to take the backseat, but when it came to creating fantasy worlds, with dragons and elves, he suddenly wanted a central role, to be the game master, the one who made up the stories with monsters and set the challenges for the other players. The boy who usually sat by himself now wanted to join in and have a say, but only about a world that existed in his and the other players' imaginations.

When Markus and his sister were around twelve and eleven, their parents divorced and their father moved out. The house became too big and expensive, so Ritva and the kids moved into an apartment. Contact with their father grew increasingly rare. The divorce was a blow to the entire family, but it really hit Markus's sister hard.

It began as innocent teenage rebellion. Anna found new friends. She began to comb her hair into a huge Mohawk. Then, one by one, she added the classic punk attributes to her look: the studded black leather jacket, the piercings, the black eye makeup. Some days, she painted sharp arrows out toward her temples. She showed up less and less often at school and at home, the fights were getting violent. Both Markus and his sister remember the time she kicked in a door at the apartment. One time Anna, who knew her brother's sensitive spot, screamed something at him about being a computer nerd, and Markus retaliated by calling her a "punk whore."

"I tried to intervene. I thought, *If I get through this with a sound mind, I'll be lucky*," says Ritva today.

One day, Markus found evidence that Anna's rebellion had taken a more serious turn. He had snuck into her room, which was something of another world for him. There lay the leather jacket, green hair spray, and records with music and lyrics no parent could understand. On one of the walls, a British flag hung askew. An old teddy bear dangled from the ceiling, a noose around its neck. And in the unmade bed, there lay a badly hidden can with a small spout and a label that said "Butane." Meant for refilling cigarette lighters, butane was known among teenagers as an easy-to-get and quick-acting intoxicant, if inhaled.

Markus was floored. Not so much because the can was proof that his sister used drugs (he was a teenager, after all, so drugs weren't a complete mystery to him) but rather by her choice of intoxicant. At school the talk was of weekend binges, but nothing he'd heard about huffing lighter fluid made it sound very enticing. Apparently the effect was about the same as you'd get from holding your breath for a very long time, but much more damaging. It just didn't sound like very much fun. Using this particular drug was, in his opinion, stupid and pointless, and he tried to make that clear to her.

It didn't work out as well as he'd hoped. Anna screamed, defended herself, and accused Markus of going through her stuff. She stiffly denied the butane was hers, or at least that she huffed it. Of course, Anna had been out of control for a while by then. Ritva had disapproved of the black, studded clothes and the punk rock. And then her daughter's interest in piercing had developed into a fascination with scarification, a form of tattoo where patterns are cut rather than inked into one's skin. But the butane was different. Ritva then knew she was losing her grip on the situation, and so she turned to social services for professional intervention.

Markus handled the chaos in his usual manner: he isolated himself. People who were close to the family can't really remember a time when Markus was seen doing anything other than sitting in front of the computer. Even today, he speaks of the computer, of code and the world of programming, as a sanctuary, a quiet place where he can be alone with his thoughts.

In order to better understand Anna's behavior, we need to tell her father's story. Birger was an addict. The drugs—mostly amphetamines—had been a part of Birger's life before the kids were born, but he stayed clean during their childhood. After Birger and Ritva's separation, however, it wasn't long before Birger went back to his old habits. Shortly after that, he left Stockholm and went to live in a small cabin out in the country, a long train trip away from his children.

Birger became increasingly isolated from the rest of the family. Ritva did her best to avoid all contact with him. One day, the family received news that he'd been arrested. He'd been involved in some kind of break-in, they were informed. Birger was sent to prison.

Today, no one in the family really remembers a trial or any specific charges; they had cut all ties with Birger. Even Markus "shut it out," as he puts it. Much later, after the prison sentence, Markus received a telephone call. He heard his dad through the receiver telling him that he was free.

"Well," Markus answered, "do you want me to feel sorry for you or something?"

Services at the City Church were beginning to feel less relevant to a teenage Markus. It was no longer so obvious to him that there was a god watching over him. The revelation didn't come through introspection or soul-searching, but through the rationale of a programmer who contemplates what is reasonable to believe in. Markus didn't lose his faith; he replaced it with logic.

Just before beginning high school, Markus, like all Swedish students, went to see the school's guidance counselor. Inside the office, he said he knew exactly what he wanted to do in life: program computer games. Few of his teenage classmates had such a clear ambition; hardly anyone else got their dreams so effectively crushed, either. Make games? Like, as a job? The guidance counselor took it as a joke and recommended the media program because, he told Markus, it had a branch that, unlike computer games, offered a bright future: print media. Dejected, Markus accepted the offer and left. Media at Tumba High School was what he got.

The school did have one major upside. Even though the courses smelled more of printing ink and thick sheets of paper than the digital world Markus loved, there was an elective in programming. Markus went to a total of two classes. During the first one, he ignored the teacher's instructions and instead programmed his own version of

Pong. The teacher took one look over Markus's shoulder and made a quick decision.

"Just come back to the last class and take the test," he said.

Markus got an A.

During the summer between his first and second years at high school, the fights at home got so bad that Anna moved out. His sister describes her following years as a complete chaos of drugs and self-destructive behavior. From the huffing she'd moved on to heavy drinking. Then she tried amphetamines, the same drug her father was hooked on. Anna became the sole member of the family to maintain any contact with papa Birger during the years he was using. She tells us today how they began to take drugs together and how she became more of a dope buddy than a daughter to him. Markus stayed in touch with his sister throughout this period, but could only look on as she fell deeper into dependency.

Markus and Ritva were now alone in the apartment. Markus had graduated from high school in Stockholm in the late 1990s, when the dot-com bubble was at its greatest and pretty much any teenager with basic computer skills could get a job at a hyped-up web agency with fancy offices. Markus's problem was not that he didn't understand his opportunities, but that he was all too aware of them. He tried working at a web agency for a short time, but thought the programming tasks were boring, so he quit. There were always other jobs out there, he figured. And there were, until the first signs that the expected giant profits from the new generation of IT companies would never materialize, and the bubble burst.

Suddenly, being a gifted, slightly introverted teenager with mounds of programming knowledge but no formal education wasn't such a promising position to be in. But then, Markus had never wanted to be a run-of-the-mill programmer at a run-of-the-mill company. He wanted to make games.

"I'm going to get rich," his sister remembers him saying once. "And then I'll take you on a helicopter ride."

But he had no plan to make it happen.

An unemployed Markus started to feel quite comfortable living at home with his mom. With both his dad and sister gone, there was plenty of room, and the place was quiet enough for him to sit undisturbed at his computer.

Ritva remembers him saying once, "Mom, I'm going to live with you my whole life." She could see how the years would pass without Markus getting either a job or an apartment. *Oh, my God, what a nightmare*, she thought. But she just smiled, and her son shuffled back into his room and sat down in front of the computer.

Ritva didn't try to throw Markus out, but she did try to at least get him out of the house during the day. Every day, she opened the free newspaper, *Metro,* and carefully read through the ads for courses. When she saw one that was for programming, she signed him up without asking him if he was interested. After a few failed attempts, she finally got Markus to go to a short course on the programming language C++.

Markus also continued working on his own games, and he'd come a long way since his first attempts with text adventures. He had become a skilled amateur coder, experimenting with small, simple games that tested new, original ideas. Markus started competing in game-development contests, where the goal was to develop a game in a short time using the least amount of code possible. It forced him to think economically—just the kind of fast-paced programming he liked so much. The aim was not to make money, and he didn't. It was more about getting attention and recognition from other amateur developers.

Luckily enough, the IT industry soon began to rise from the ruins of the crash. Markus took an opportunity to work at the fringes of the gaming industry, at a company called Gamefederation. It was not a game-developing company—Gamefederation worked with systems for game distribution. But now and then, Markus would get the chance to create small game prototypes in order to test a system's functions. These creations haven't been saved for posterity, but for the first time Markus was getting paid for something that at least resembled game programming, and that, he liked.

When Markus was hired at Gamefederation, another developer, Rolf Jansson, had already started working there. Rolf quickly became Markus's closest colleague, despite their drastically different backgrounds. Unlike Markus, Rolf already had substantial work experience. Before ending up at Gamefederation with Markus, he had been a consultant at IBM—a dream job for many. The pay had been great and, being a successful employee of one of the world's largest IT companies, his future would have been secure. Nevertheless, Rolf, just like Markus, dreamed of working with games.

Rolf remembers Markus as being shy and quiet, but a nice guy. It was when the two of them began talking about games that Markus lit up, and they had a lot to talk about. Markus got Rolf to play *Counter-Strike*, and Rolf showed Markus his favorite games. Soon, the two of them began staying late after work, playing multiplayer games on the company's network. Sometimes they sacrificed a lunch and went over to The Science Fiction Bookstore, in Stockholm's Gamla stan (the Old Town), where they bought cards for Magic: The Gathering. Between game sessions, they would talk at length about what was missing from the games available on the market, and together they could envision the perfect game and figure out what it was that the next hit game needed.

Markus stayed at Gamefederation for four years. He then got the chance to enter the game industry for real when he interviewed for a then-unknown company, Midasplayer. The little he'd heard about it was promising. At Midasplayer, each developer was responsible for his or her own games. On top of that, Markus liked that the company focused on making small games to be played online. It sounded like what he'd been doing on his own for years without earning a cent. Everything seemed to be falling into place; they just needed to hire him.

CHAPTER 4

GAMES WORTH BILLIONS

"DO YOU KNOW ActionScript?"

The job interview at Midasplayer began really badly. Markus couldn't dodge such a direct question, and the only honest answer was a straight no. He had experimented with most existing programming languages used to create small online games, but not ActionScript. Unfortunately, that was the only one used at the company where he wanted to work.

Markus got the job anyway, an indication of how quickly Midasplayer was growing at the time. Each day, the line of commuters from the subway station to Midasplayer's main office on Kungsholms Square in Stockholm grew longer. The year was 2004 and the company was just a year old.

Markus had to spend his first week at his new job learning ActionScript before he could begin working on his own projects. He mostly sat quietly staring into his screen, partly because he was focused, and partly because he had quickly noticed that the powers that be at his place of work were nothing like him. He began, for the first time, to glimpse the contours of a gaming world quite different from what he had dreamt of since childhood.

To understand how he felt, you need to lift your gaze a bit and look more closely at the professional gaming industry. In Stockholm, one company exemplifies the Goliaths of that world better than anything else.

On the other side of the inner city from Midasplayer's offices are the headquarters of the game studio DICE. On dark evenings, boats entering Stockholm from the south are greeted by a brightly lit neon sign displaying the company's logo, high up on the glass facade of the building next to the Slussen locks. At that exclusive address, nine floors above the street, some of Sweden's most successful export items have been created. From inside the offices you can view Gamla stan and the sea approach to Stockholm through panoramic windows.

DICE is owned by Electronic Arts, one the largest video game publishers in the world. Daily life there is markedly different from the amateur programming that Markus was used to. The company's games are products, adapted to target audiences down to the smallest detail, backed by billions of dollars in marketing, and delivered with elaborate planning in order to boost the parent company's quarterly profits and stock market value. DICE's cash cow is the game series *Battlefield*, a realistic, tactical war simulator that has sold over 50 million copies. The first part in the series, *Battlefield 1942*, was released in 2002. Since then, DICE has honed and tweaked the concept in sixteen different sequels, with wars being alternately staged in Vietnam, the Europe of WWII, and a fictional future conflict between the United States and Russia.

In late 2011, the company was gearing up to launch its latest title in the series: *Battlefield 3*. The release would be an internationally acclaimed event in the gaming world, as elaborate as a major Hollywood premiere, coordinated by an international team of marketers and PR experts. For several months, expectations were raised with ad campaigns and articles in gaming magazines. Particular emphasis was put on the game's new, completely redesigned engine, which allowed DICE to create a more realistic war experience than ever before. "All the sights, sounds, and action of real-world incursions," the ads bragged. In trailers, backed by grinding heavy-metal guitars, virtually photorealistic soldiers could be seen rushing around through urban environments that were promptly shot to pieces.

At the same time, the stock market was massaged with gilt-edged information about the new game. Electronic Arts' well-dressed CEO, John Riccitiello, spoke often and inspirationally about how *Battlefield 3* would push up Electronic Arts' market value. The competition was *Call of Duty*, a war game from archrival Activision Blizzard.

"*Call of Duty* did 400 million dollars in revenue on day one. Battlefield 3 is designed to take that game down," John Riccitiello told the audience at the Ad Age conference in New York.

Battlefield 3 was released simultaneously in tens of thousands of game shops the world over. Many of the most devoted fans stood in line for hours, and several stores stayed open for midnight launches. In preparation for the premiere at the Webhallen video game store in Stockholm, extras dressed as soldiers entertained the waiting crowd with fights and staged robbery attempts. DICE employees celebrated the release by renting out one of Stockholm's oldest and finest restaurant-nightclubs and throwing a giant party, where they toasted each other with champagne while the pop star September entertained them.

During its first week in stores, *Battlefield 3* sold more than 5 million copies. The financial people at Electronic Arts established that the game had added about $37 million to the company's coffers—significantly more money than *Avatar*, one of the most lucrative films ever, earned during its first weekend in the theaters. For the uninitiated, the numbers may seem sky-high, but they were exactly in line with what the bosses at Electronic Arts had predicted. *Battlefield 3* was just more proof that computer games are big business.

In 2010, computer games were sold to the tune of $46.7 billion. That's more than double the total amount of music sold, $16.4 billion. If you believe the industry's own statistics, the consumer demographics are a far cry from the usual picture of gamers as mainly young men and boys. Four out of ten players in the United States are women. Three out of ten are over fifty years old, and only one out of ten is a boy under seventeen years old. Today, gaming is one of the world's largest, most appreciated, and most demographically widespread forms of entertainment.

The CEO at DICE at the time of *Battlefield 3*'s release was Karl-Magnus Troedsson. For over twenty years, his career has run parallel to the development of the Swedish gaming industry. In the late 1990s, right after completing his studies at the college in Gävle, he was hired by the game company Unique Development Studios (UDS). The first game he worked on was *Mall Maniacs*, an advertising game developed for a Swedish grocery store chain and McDonald's, in which the player's task was to fill a shopping cart with advertised items as fast as possible. A couple of years later, he began working at Digital

Illusions, which later became DICE. Sweden, particularly the Stockholm region, had by then established itself as one of Europe's most prominent centers of game development. Today, Swedish games pull in almost $1.4 billion in yearly sales for the large companies. A big chunk of that money goes to DICE.

Today, the situation is very different from the experimental workshops of the early years. Karl Magnus Troedsson calls it "mature" and "more professional." Others would probably use words like *cold* and *unforgiving*. Enormous sums of money are invested in each game that actually makes it to market, and the demands on a successful studio like DICE are immense. New games have to place either first, second, or third on the ranking lists. Anything less is considered a flop.

The largest games publishers, such as Electronic Arts, are listed on the stock exchange and run, like other huge companies, according to quarterly reports and the expectations of the market. They navigate using Excel spreadsheets full of sales prognoses and cost analyses. Publishers like Electronic Arts are the most powerful in the video game industry. They finance the game developers' projects and decide whether or not a game will get produced. They also control the enormous budgets needed to market a popular game—a general rule is that just as much money is spent on advertising and marketing as on the programming itself and, in extreme cases, such as that of *Battlefield 3*, several times more. And it's the publishers alone who have access to the distribution and production contacts that are needed to press millions of CD or DVD disks and then ship them to stores throughout the world. The five largest game publishers—Nintendo, Sony, Microsoft, Activision Blizzard, and Electronic Arts—accounted for about 70 percent of the turnover in the industry in 2008.

The enormous budgets and gruesome deadlines that mark large productions engender predictability and standardization. That doesn't necessarily mean bad quality. For example, *Battlefield 3* has been praised as one of the most impressive games of 2011. There is, however, less room to test new ideas. For a nonplayer, there is very little that separates *Battlefield 1942*—the first edition of DICE's series, released in 2002—from the latest version. Huge productions tend, like giant Hollywood films, to build upon proven concepts that appeal to as large an audience as possible. Sports games, which can be updated each year to reflect the latest season's player lineups, are among the most profitable in the business and are produced assembly-line style by the big publishers.

From the point of view of publishers, experimental game concepts are risky. Why try something different when another *Battlefield* with better graphics and even more impressive explosions is almost guaranteed to sell at least as well as its predecessor? New ideas mean untested ground and therefore greater risk that the investment won't pay off. Only a fraction of the thousands of game productions that are initiated each year ever reach the top of the sales-ranking lists. Though it's the publishers taking the economic risk, the resulting failure or success is most felt at the development level. New opportunities materialize for the studios that succeed, then more money from the publisher and greater freedom to determine the tone of the next project. For those who fail, one single wrong turn can mean disaster.

That was something that brothers Bo and Ulf Andersson learned firsthand in the summer of 2008. They were two guys from Huddinge, outside of Stockholm, whose names were on the lips of everyone in the gaming industry. In just a couple of years, they had taken the game studio Grin from being a small newcomer to one of Sweden's most talked about. The company worked on several large games, among them a hyped-up new interpretation of the eighties classic *Bionic Commando* (commissioned by Japanese Capcom), and a game based on the movie *Wanted* (to be published by French game company Ubisoft). Grin's breakthrough came in 2006, with the war game *Ghost Recon Advanced Warfighter*. The game was hailed by the critics, became a retail success, and was celebrated with expensive champagne at the corporate office. Some of the gaming world's absolute top people had their eyes on Grin and flew to Stockholm to listen to the Andersson brothers' visions of the future.

A few years later, there were rumors in the business that Square Enix itself, one of Japan's most esteemed video game publishers, had hired Grin for a high-stakes prestige project. The Andersson brothers had been given the task of developing the next installment of the iconic gaming series *Final Fantasy*. It was a huge deal. Japanese publishers seldom use Western game studios for their most important titles. Being asked to work on the next sequel of Japan's most famous video game series was, for a relatively unproven Swedish developer like Grin, comparable to two newly graduated architects from Sweden being asked to redesign the Sydney Opera House. Grin expanded swiftly and hired new people. By the end of 2008, the company had nearly three hundred employees and offices in far-off places like Barcelona and Jakarta.

Then things took a turn for the worse. Neither *Bionic Commando* nor *Wanted* received the warm welcome that Grin had expected, right when the financial crisis made game-players think twice before opening their wallets. Sales were so-so. Not a disaster, but not good enough for Grin to count on making back the enormous amounts of money they had invested. Their Japanese employers began to worry.

Just before summer 2009, they received the fateful news; Square Enix was withdrawing the *Final Fantasy* contract from Grin, mumbling something about deficient quality, and canceled all payments. The Andersson brothers could only look on as their life's work began to fall apart. The company they had devoted their lives to building was impossible to save. In the summer of 2009, Grin filed for bankruptcy and 250 people lost their jobs.

2009 was a sobering year for the Swedish gaming industry. Several years of astronomical growth were followed by a major decline. Total sales in the industry fell by 17 percent. Since then, the figures have improved, but the fantastic growth of the first years of the twenty-first century has completely vanished.

With constantly ballooning budgets and increasing competition for players' cash, it's easy to see, in retrospect, the signs that the gaming industry was painting itself into a corner. There's nothing wrong with the games—interest in computer games is greater than ever, and Swedish-designed and developed games are internationally acclaimed. However, there is evidence that the traditional publishing model, favoring large, lavish game productions at the expense of smaller, bolder ideas and innovation, had perhaps grown about as large and profitable as it was going to get.

This is where Midasplayer, into whose offices Markus first stepped in the fall of 2004, comes into play. Their business concept contradicts many of the industry's established truths. The company develops only the kind of small, simple, web-based games that Markus was hired to design more of, games played on computers, cell phones, or on a tablet, either through an app or on the website King.com. Midasplayer offers innumerable versions of popular board games and card games, along with variations of well-known arcade games and puzzles. Most of them can be played free of charge—provided the player agrees to watch a few ads. Others cost a few dollars a month to play. In many of the games, you can even bet on yourself and win a few bucks if you're good.

Today, Midasplayer is one of Sweden's largest gaming companies. In 2012, it had more than a hundred employees, tens of millions of players every day, and nearly $14 million in sales. The company is in many ways the antithesis of how a traditional game studio like DICE operates. It has no publishers or stores acting as middlemen—games are bought online and the players' money goes right into the pockets of the game developers. Indicative of the potential that investors see in the model, the gaming giant Zynga, specializing in Facebook games and perhaps Midasplayer's biggest competitor, had an estimated value of nearly $9 billion when it went public in December 2011. Most experts with an eye on the gaming industry feel that it's the small, simple productions like the ones created by Zynga and Midasplayer that will reap the future profits. And it was in this corner of the industry that Markus began his career as a professional game developer.

CHAPTER 5

"THEY JUST DON'T GET IT."

MARKUS'S FIRST FEW months at Midasplayer were good. Fantastic, even. Every morning, he got himself out of bed and out the door, to the commuter train and into Midasplayer's office in central Stockholm. It was a dream job for a young game developer. Hundreds of thousands of people played the games he and his colleagues put out on the web. Besides, he was well paid.

Markus was one of the first game developers to be hired

at Midasplayer. Soon there were a few others, until around twenty people shared the office. Everyone worked according to the same, well-practiced model: each individual game was developed by a group of two to eight people and never took more than four months to finish. It was a fast and, more important, very cheap way to develop games. Markus liked working fast and, as a developer, having some degree of control during the whole process.

But soon he realized that it wasn't a love of quality games that determined which projects he and the other programmers were assigned. The management at Midasplayer had an ice-cold mathematical approach to their products. Games that immediately earned a lot of money or showed a high virality (Midasplayer-speak for spreading quickly via recommendations among friends and acquaintances) were praised as hits. The company quickly put the developers to work on sequels, enhanced with better graphics and new features, to entice the player to spend even more money and time.

At the same time, innovative projects, usually the games Markus liked, were quickly brushed aside as uninteresting. Midasplayer's successes came from an extreme reach—several million players who each paid a small sum—and a narrow concept of what they considered appropriate to produce. All the games were built on a few, well-established concepts. Card games and board games were popular, as well as clones of arcade classics like

Puzzle Bobble (a "bubble shooter" or "bubble spinner," as they were called). Many titles were almost identical to one another, differing only in graphic themes, sound effects, and scoring systems. Trying new things was just not a part of Midasplayer's business plan.

For Markus, that insight was depressing. Sometimes it felt more like he worked in a casino, responsible only for trimming the poker tables and roulette games, than in the world of game creation that he'd dreamt about.

But there were advantages to having a stable job. Just before he started at Midasplayer, Markus was finally able to break his promise (or threat?) to live at home with his mom for the rest of his life. She wasn't sure why he'd changed his mind, but one day Markus came home and told her that he'd found an apartment in Sollentuna, north of Stockholm, that he wanted to buy. The place wasn't extraordinary, but at least it was his. When the paperwork was complete, Markus took his computer, clothes, and the rest of his stuff, gave Mom a hug and vanished.

It's common for parents to visit their children's first own home and be appalled. Ritva describes Markus's apartment in Sollentuna as a disaster zone: The bed unmade, the floor covered with dirty clothes and empty soda bottles. And everywhere, games. There were floppy disks, CDs, and game boxes in a glorious mess. The only thing that wasn't covered with a thick layer of dust was Markus's computer. When Ritva came to visit, she couldn't resist going over the place with a vacuum cleaner and a wet rag, scrubbing away the worst of the grime.

"It's like he doesn't see it. For him, it's completely irrelevant if it's a mess," says a person close to Markus, who often visited him in Sollentuna.

While Markus had moved out of the house, gotten a steady job, and was making money, his sister was sinking deeper into drugs. There were times when Anna was homeless and living on the street. The siblings kept in touch, and Anna describes her brother as the only fixed point in her life at that time. But they were seeing less of each other, and when they did meet, it was usually about money. Markus hated to see Anna losing control, but he didn't know what to do to help her. Giving her money was meaningless, he knew that, but when she asked for it, he seldom had the heart to say no. Anna remembers one of the many instances when she called on her brother at home. Markus took a five-hundred-kronor bill ($70) from his wallet and held it out to his sister.

"Take this now and you'll never get anything else from me," he said.

Anna swallowed her pride, took the money, and disappeared.

Perhaps his messy family life was one reason why Markus clung to his job. In spite of everything, it was still the best job he'd ever had and besides, he really liked the other programmers. Markus always describes himself as quiet and shy, but if you ask his colleagues, a different image emerges. When with his closest coworkers, Markus was happy and open. He was the one who made sure they went for beers after work or got together for a couple of rounds of *Counter-Strike* or *Team Fortress 2* during their lunch break. People at work shared the same interests, the same deeply rooted fascination with computer games and programming, and were just as nerdy as he was.

Markus found a better outlet for his ambitions outside of work. He and Rolf Jansson had already realized their plan to develop a game together. It was titled *Wurm Online*, and it was an extremely ambitious project for two amateur developers. An online role-playing game, *Wurm Online* was a spacious and open world, where a large number of players took part simultaneously. The game differed from others of the same genre (the immensely popular *World of Warcraft*, for example) mainly in its openness. The world born of Markus and Rolf's vision was one where the players were free to change anything they wanted—to build houses, dig mineshafts, earn money, or wage war on one another, for example.

When Markus began working for Midasplayer, *Wurm Online* had already been live for a couple of months. The two friends spent almost all their free time on the game, thinking, planning, and programming together until the early morning hours. They didn't make any money from it, at least not yet, but for Markus and Rolf it was enough just to see how increasing numbers of players found their way to their fantasy world and chose to stay inside it. For Markus, *Wurm Online* was a creative refuge. There, he could test his own ideas and develop the game as he wished, without asking his managers at Midasplayer for permission.

With time, Markus became a knowledgeable and experienced game programmer, particularly with the Java programming language. With experience came the task of teaching newcomers at the firm. Management often had to contend with the fact that those who showed up for the job interviews didn't always know a lot about game development. Most often, they figured it would work out anyway and counted on the more experienced developers to take the new talent under their wings.

Among the new talent was Jakob Porser, who had recently become a father and had been a consultant before his job vanished in the dot-com crash a couple of years earlier. After that he took a course in creative programming at the college in Gävle—the same course that DICE's CEO, Karl Magnus Troedsson, had completed barely ten years earlier. Jakob then moved to Stockholm to find work, and Midasplayer hired him. To learn more, he was assigned to sit next to Markus. With his dark mop of hair, his rectangular glasses, and his quick speech, Jakob seemed very different from Markus. Besides, he had a baby to support, which meant that he felt differently about his new job. Earning a paycheck was his highest priority.

But like Markus, Jakob loved computer games, and the two programmers immediately hit it off. They had the same interests and sense of humor and could end up sitting for hours at work, absorbed in conversations about obscure computer games. As with Rolf Jansson a couple of years earlier, Markus and Jakob had a shared enthusiasm for Magic: The Gathering, and when they weren't playing the game themselves, they were discussing ways to improve it.

Markus told Jakob about his experiences with *Wurm Online*. Jakob listened with interest and told Markus about the game he dreamed of developing. It would be a kind of digital version of Magic: The Gathering, where the cards were stored in the computer and the players could meet in matches over the Internet; a strategy game in a fantasy world, but also inspired by the card collecting and trading that characterized Magic. Markus loved it. After work they'd go to a pizza shop and remain there until late into the evenings, fleshing out Jakob's roughly outlined ideas, discussing game mechanics, and polishing their plans for the future.

Markus also met his future wife at Midasplayer. One day at work, he passed by a conference room on his way to his office and saw through the glass wall a short woman sitting with her back toward him. One of the managers was on the other side of the desk. It was obviously a job interview. The girl being interviewed was Elin, and she was hired a few weeks later as an online community coordinator. Her job was to manage the company's contact with users of Midasplayer's casino games, making sure that everything worked and helping players solve any issues.

Elin's first day at Midasplayer was June 1, which also happened to be Markus's birthday. That evening, all the programmers went out to celebrate, and Elin came along. Markus had already decided he wanted to get to know her and now, with a couple of beers under his belt, he mustered the courage and introduced himself. The exchange must have looked comical—Elin is as short and thin as Markus is tall and large—but the two remained in each other's company the whole evening. They talked about computer games, and even though Elin was no programmer, she was just as devoted to games as Markus. They even had the same tastes.

Computer games brought Markus and Elin closer during their initial friendship. Every day at lunch they connected their computers and tried to kill each other in *Team Fortress 2* (Markus won most of the games then, says Elin, but she makes it very clear that today she gets at least as many points as he does.) They soon began spending more time together; they went out after work, then out to dinner, then to the amusement park Gröna

Lund. His colleagues soon realized that Markus and the girl from the casino department were a thing.

Elin also became the person Markus went to when he needed to vent his irritation over the managers at Midasplayer. It was increasingly obvious that he wasn't happy at work. He liked being responsible for every aspect of a game project, from idea to implementation, and it drove him crazy having click statistics and profit as the only goals to strive for.

"They just don't get it," he would say to Elin after work. "They're idiots."

When Markus began working at Midasplayer, company policy forbade employees from making money on independently developed games. That wasn't particularly odd; few employers like to have their employees moonlighting with what can be seen as a competitive enterprise. However, during Midasplayer's first year, no one took the rule seriously. Besides *Wurm Online*, which Markus had worked on before he was even hired at the company, he kept developing his own little games in his free time, mostly as a way to explore the ideas he wasn't allowed to pursue at work.

Management didn't really think that Markus's amateur coding was a problem. It didn't disturb his workday at the company, and there was nothing to complain about in

Markus Persson and Elin Zetterstrand playing video games at the Mojang office in Stockholm. Photo courtesy of Elin Zetterstrand. Photo by Joshua

Markus's performance. They just looked the other way. However, the more Midasplayer grew, the more strictly the rules were enforced, and Markus felt it firsthand one day in the fall of 2008. He had just finished his latest hobby project, a game called *Blast Passage*. It was a kind of combination of two classic arcade games, *Bomberman* and *Gauntlet*, and for those who know their gaming history, the result was both cleverly allusive and appealing. *Blast Passage* was simple, fun, and full of winks to the old eighties titles that inspired it. Not without certain pride, Markus sent out an e-mail to the other employees at Midasplayer with a link, encouraging them to try it out. The reaction was not what Markus expected.

Versions of what actually happened differ, depending on whom you ask. Markus describes how, almost immediately after sending the e-mail, he was called into a conference room. There, he was severely reprimanded by Lars Markgren, director of the company and the person who had founded Midasplayer a couple of years earlier. Lars Markgren reminded him of the rules in his contract, emphasizing that all games Markus developed belonged to Midasplayer and that this clause applied to *Blast Passage*. Markus received a warning and the orders to shape up.

Lars Markgren has another recollection of what happened. What Markus calls a reprimand, Lars describes as a discussion. Markus had permission to work with *Wurm Online* in his free time, says Lars Markgren, but

Blast Passage was too similar to the games Midasplayer developed. Lars suggested that Markus adapt the game to Midasplayer customers and release it to the public. A version of *Blast Passage* was uploaded onto King.com shortly thereafter. It never became a huge success; the typical player at King.com isn't particularly well versed in gaming history and prefers a few moments of recreation to clever references. Midaplayer customers just weren't interested in *Blast Passage*.

The conflict had a huge impact on Markus. His freedom to work on his own projects had been perhaps the main reason why he hadn't left Midasplayer earlier.

"Why should I stay here?" Markus asked himself.

In moments like that, he liked to think back to the discussions he'd had with Jakob. The two of them had become more and more convinced that they wanted to start their own game studio in due time. Markus now had experience developing a game of his own; his years with *Wurm Online* had showed him it could be done if you applied yourself enough. Also, Jakob's idea (the basis of the game that would later become *Scrolls*) felt too promising to just set aside, and they had several other ideas they wanted to sink their teeth into. However, with the new, stricter Midasplayer rules, the possibility felt remote.

No matter how much thought Markus gave it, he couldn't figure out how to make the equation add up. He could give notice and throw himself wholeheartedly into his own games—but then he wouldn't be able to afford food or the roof over his head. Or he could stay at Midasplayer and continue to live well on the money he made, and totally abandon his dream of creating the games he really loved.

Shortly thereafter, Markus was given a way out. He interviewed for and accepted a position at Avalanche, a game studio with over two hundred employees and some of the Swedish gaming industry's most ambitious titles in their portfolio. Their hit game, *Just Cause 2*, released in 2010, cost over $3 million to develop and is regarded, along with the *Battlefield* series, as one of the Swedish game industry's most elaborate projects ever.

Many young game developers dream of working for a studio like Avalanche. Markus hated it. Each morning, he felt like a factory worker on his way to his place on the assembly line. The project he worked on was so huge he hardly knew what the end result would look like. As a programmer, he had only sporadic contact with the game's design team, which meant that he could work for days on animation tools for game characters without even knowing how the character in the game would look. He felt irrelevant, like a tiny cog in a machine so large that he didn't understand how it worked. Markus could only stomach two weeks of it. Then he gave his notice and left, returning hat in hand to his old managers and job at Midasplayer.

In early 2009 someone threw Markus another lifeline. An acquaintance at a programming forum tipped off Markus about a job at Jalbum. The small, newly launched company had developed a platform for creating photo albums online. The responsibilities listed for the job were about as far away from game development as a programmer could get, but at that point it didn't matter to Markus; he just needed to get away from Midasplayer.

Markus sent in his application and was called for an interview. On the spot, Markus made his own demands. He was only interested in working at Jalbum on the condition that his employer would not interfere with his hobby and would let him continue developing games in his free time. Of course, his future boss shrugged his shoulders and said yes. Carl Manneh, CEO at Jalbum, couldn't care less about what Markus did in his free time, as long as he came to work on time and did what was expected of him while he was there.

With an offer from Jalbum secured, it didn't take long for Markus to again quit his job at Midasplayer. But before he did, he discussed the matter with Jakob. Immediately after leaving Midasplayer, Markus intended to sit down and start developing a new game, he said, and if, contrary to expectation, he succeeded in making any money at it, the two friends would proceed with their plans and start a game studio together.

Markus's decision to leave was a direct consequence

of Midasplayer's refusal to let him develop games in his free time. However, it was also because Markus's perception of the gaming world differed fundamentally from that of the bosses at Midasplayer. To them, the games were products for consumption; they could just as well have been selling detergent or toilet paper or candy. To Markus, the games themselves were the be-all and end-all. If he wasn't allowed to work on the projects he liked, he might as well do something else.

Markus was not alone in harboring these sentiments. Just as in the film or music industries, the conflict between commercial success and creative freedom has always been present in the gaming world. Midasplayer had grown into a large, established company, focusing on tried-and-true concepts that would generate the most profit from each hour of development. *Minecraft*, which would grow into one of the most successful games of the decade, was born from a different tradition. In order to understand how it happened, you need to move the spotlight away from the arena of commercial mass production and onto another, completely different, and often overlooked corner of the gaming world.

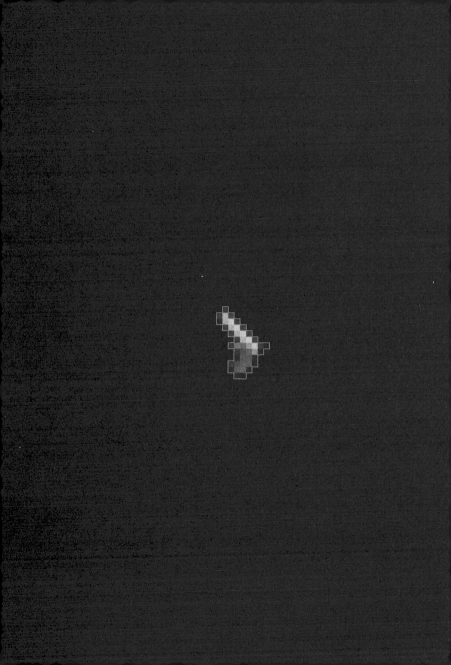

CHAPTER 6

MACHO MEN WITH BIG GUNS

ON THE EVENING of July 27, 2008, more than fifteen young men sat sequestered in a basement room in Skövde, Sweden, just a stone's throw from the city's college. Twenty-eight hours later, they would emerge into the daylight, one summer night poorer, dozens of new computer games richer. The event was called No More Sweden and it was the first of what would become a recurring event in the Swedish gaming world.

Jens Bergensten. Art by Ethan Thornton. Photo courtesy of Mojang.

In attendance were Jens "Jeb" Bergensten, then mostly known for the strategy game *Harvest: Massive Encounter*, and Nicklas "Nifflas" Nygren, who'd created the popular platform games *Knytt* and *Knytt Stories*, based on the character Knyttet (Toffle, in English) in Tove Jansson's *Moomin* books. Erik Svedäng, developer of the prizewinning adventure game *Blueberry Garden* and the arcade game *Shot Shot Shoot* for Apple's iPad was there, and of course Jonatan "Cactus" Söderström, a twenty-six-year-old self-taught programmer from Gothenburg, known to be unbelievably prolific (in just a few years he had developed and self-published more than forty games, with names like *Burn the Trash*; *Shotgun Ninja*; *Clean Asia!*; and *Keyboard Drumset Fucking Werewolf*, an interactive music video for the Gothenburg post–punk rock band Fucking Werewolf Asso). The guys in the basement all belonged to the world of self-financed game developers who have always lived alongside the mainstream industry. In a nutshell, the cream of the Swedish indie game scene had gathered to meet for three days to mingle, swap stories, and create games.

The "cream" is a relative concept. The Swedish indie scene is a narrow subculture kept alive by a small number of enthusiasts. Fifteen people in a basement in Skövde doesn't sound particularly glamorous, but if someone in the future decides to track down the roots of the Swedish indie game scene, he or she will probably discover a programmer meet-up just like this one.

Twenty-two-year-old Erik Svedäng took the initiative and organized the first No More Sweden. He had been programming games for as long as he could remember, and for several years had wanted to attend the Independent Games Festival in San Francisco. However, it's hard just to scratch out a living as an independent game developer, and in 2008 Svedäng was forced to accept that, once again, he couldn't afford plane tickets to San Francisco that year. So he decided to organize his own festival instead. All he needed was a venue; finding enthusiastic game developers to fill it wouldn't be a problem.

After the programming contest, in which everyone present got twenty-eight hours to create a game, there was an awards ceremony. Svedäng and his friend Petri Purho won in the categories "Most Next-Gen" and "Most Erotic," with the creation *You Have to Knock the Penis*, a precision game they've described as a "feminist statement." The prize for "Best Game" went to Jonatan "Cactus" Söderström, for *Stench Mechanics*. Since then, No More Sweden has taken place every year, and the number of participants keeps growing.

Both Erik Svedäng and Nicklas Nygren work full-time developing games and selling them on the Internet. In contrast, Jonatan Söderström gives his games away online and lives off donations. By indie standards, they are all successful. They don't make big money, but all of them agree it's better than working for a mainstream game company like DICE. Nicklas Nygren feels big game studios lead to creative stagnation.

"Walk into any game shop and look at the boxes. It's the same thing everywhere, just macho men with big guns shooting at other macho men. It's all stereotype and a real drag," he says.

"Of course, there are big productions that break the pattern and do fantastic things, but for the most part, it feels like the whole industry is making games for teenage boys."

All three identify the freedom to transform their own ideas into reality as their main driving force. Of course, sometimes it's hard to make ends meet, but in exchange, indie developers have full control over their creations, from the graphics and sound, to design, to game mechanics. You have room to experiment and can complete a product in a relatively short time, without having to listen to the views of other developers or anxious publishing representatives.

"If you have a really clear idea of what you want to do, it's no fun to compromise. I want to do my own projects, not just work on a small part of a huge game," says Jonatan Söderström.

Most indie developers agree that interest in small, different, and innovative game concepts is growing. With the right conditions, it's only a matter of time before more games rooted in the indie scene will reach a larger audience. According to Nicklas Nygren, "As the game industry grew, it left a hole in its wake. During the Nintendo era, there were no megasized development teams and budgets. I believe that many people long for the simpler and more experimental games of that time. That's what makes indie games work so well today. We fill that void."

The world of Nicklas Nygren and the rest in that basement in Skövde bears strong resemblances to the origins of the gaming industry, found in the early computer culture of the 1970s and '80s, and especially in the very popular (at that time) demo scene. A demo is a kind of programmed piece of artwork, combining sound and moving images into a visually impressive demonstration. The purpose of a demo was mainly to showcase a programmer's coding skills in creating visual effects. Back then, before user-friendly programs made it possible for anyone to create digital animations, such work was complicated and time-consuming.

Demo programmers would often work in inventively named groups, and compete against other groups to try and create the most impressive works. Rival groups would meet up and exhibit their creations at demoparties, a kind of predecessor to today's gaming and computer festivals. Several Scandinavian groups became famous through demoparties—Hackerence and Dreamhack, in Sweden; The Gathering, in Norway; Assembly, in Finland. These events established networks and began collaborations, giving rise to the largest export giants of the Swedish game industry. DICE has its roots in a demogroup called The Silents; Starbreeze, who developed the acclaimed games *The Chronicles of Riddick: Escape from Butcher Bay* and *The Darkness*, was formed from the group Triton; and the Finnish group Remedy, known mostly for the *Alan Wake* and *Max Payne*, has its origin in the demogroup Future Crew.

When the very first computer games were being created, development was pretty much all small-scale. *Spacewar!*, released in 1962, is considered one of the world's first computer games. It was a hobby project for programmers Steve Russell, Martin Graetz, and Wayne Wiitanen working on the PDP-1 at the Massachusetts Institute of Technology. Before Atari mass-produced *Pong* and it became a global success, programmer Allan Alcorn had written the game as a school assignment in 1972. Likewise *Tetris*, perhaps the world's most famous game, was written by a Russian programmer, Alexey Pajitnov, in his free time, with the help of two colleagues at the Russian Academy of Sciences in Moscow. Compared to today's games, these were very modest productions, with simple graphics and mechanics. Putting three hundred game developers to work for several years was unheard of—what in the world would they all do with all that time?

Not until games were packaged and sold in retail shops did the gaming industry in its present form begin to take shape. In the early 1970s, as game consoles made their way into homes, the emerging power structures became even more evident. Printing floppy disks, cassettes, boxes, and manuals was expensive. Producing console games demanded long and complicated copyright agreements with hardware manufacturers. Professional publishers were needed to take care of the paperwork and provide the capital so programmers could concentrate on creating games. And as game consoles became more powerful and games more numerous, developers' financial resources grew into the budgets of today, often totaling more than $100 million per title.

It's tempting but incorrect to describe the history of the game industry as a classic David and Goliath saga, with the crass, capitalist corporate interests in one corner and the idealistic indie scene in the other. In reality, the indie scene has always lived in a kind of symbiotic relationship with the established gaming industry, like a creatively brilliant but impossibly unbusinesslike experimental greenhouse. Those who wanted to make game design their career and not just a hobby haven't had many options to do so, except by applying to work on one of the giant companies' multimillion-dollar productions.

Lately, though, modern forms of distribution have given independent developers new ways to make money.

As is often the case, Apple is a good starting point. In the summer of 2008, the company's legendary CEO Steve Jobs stood onstage at the company's main office in Cupertino, California. That morning, he wasn't presenting a new cell phone or computer. Instead, on the agenda was an update of iPhone's operating system, with a special focus on developers.

After Jobs demonstrated the telephone's new security functions and improved e-mail support, it was time for the big news: App Store. Apple was turning the iPhone into a shop. It would be a marketplace where anyone could sell games and applications to millions of iPhone users around the world. To demonstrate the excellence of the new technology, Electronic Arts' boss Travis Boatman was invited onto the stage. He showed the audience an iPhone-compatible version of the game *Spore* and showered praise on Apple's invention.

It should be noted that Apple was, in fact, far from first. In typical Steve Jobs style, Apple's mobile store was more like refining an already established model and applying it to its own market. The idea had come from the game industry, which had taken the first steps toward online sales almost five years earlier. In 2003, Valve, known primarily for the game series *Half-Life*, launched the distribution platform Steam. It soon became the market leader and is today the natural home for PC games distributed over the Internet. In 2004, Microsoft launched the Xbox Live Arcade platform, and in 2006 Sony started its PlayStation Store. Nintendo was last out of the gate, releasing WiiWare in May 2008. When the App Store saw the light of day, all four major game platforms already had digital distribution channels on the market.

Today, Electronic Arts probably feels a little left behind. The company has of course reaped huge success on Apple's platforms, but the App Store and other digital distribution platforms have proven most advantageous for small-scale, independent game developers. In a telling move, Travis Boatman left the company in 2012 to join Midasplayer-rival Zynga. During the last few years, the portion of digitally sold games has increased greatly, and in 2010 it totaled one fourth of the game industry's overall turnover. Many of the most popular games are still released by traditional publishers, but the move to digital distribution has also revolutionized the conditions for indie developers. Both Apple and Valve take 30 percent of a game's sales, and the rest of the money goes directly to the developer. That's a large piece to pay, it may seem, but keeping 70 percent of the retail price is but a dream for those studios working in accordance with the traditional publishing model. The most important change brought about by digital distribution, it turns out, is not lower costs for the publishers—it's that the publishers are no longer needed.

CHAPTER 7

"THIS IS WAY TOO MUCH FUN. I BUILT A BRIDGE."

FOR MOST PEOPLE, the colorful numbers and letters that filled the computer screen would be completely baffling, but Markus felt right at home. The game was called *Dwarf Fortress* and it had become a cult favorite in indie circles. Markus had downloaded it to try it out himself and watched, entranced by the simple text world drawn up in front of him.

A couple of weeks had passed since Markus started working at Jalbum and his thoughts were circling full speed around the game he'd promised himself he'd work on. Like when he was a child and would run home from school to his LEGO pieces, he now spent almost all his free time in front of his home computer. He combed the Internet in search of inspiration for his project; the heavy labor—the coding—could begin only after he figured out what kind of game he wanted to create. The idea for *Minecraft* began to take shape in his encounter with *Dwarf Fortress*.

In *Dwarf Fortress* the player is tasked with helping a group of dwarf warriors build a fortress in bedrock. The player controls a group of dwarves that can each be put to various tasks (chopping down trees, mining ore from the mountain, cooking, making furniture, fishing, for example) or made to protect the fortress from monsters such as evil vampires, giant spiders, trolls, and wolves. The basic game mechanics are similar to many other strategy games—*The Sims*, for example, where the player manages a household or the Facebook game *Farmville*, where the objective is to get a farm to flourish. But *Dwarf Fortress* is different from most other games of the genre in a couple of ways.

First of all, the graphics are highly stylized. The *Dwarf Fortress* game world is completely made up of letters, numbers, and other symbols that can be typed on a regular keyboard. In this game, a terrifying giant spider is not a detailed 3-D model but a simple gray letter *S*. Minerals to be mined from the rock are represented by the British pound sign, beds are pale-yellow crosses, grassy mead-ows and trees are green dots and triangles, and so on. Small, smiling faces of different colors represent the dwarves. Many *Dwarf Fortress* players maintain that the simple graphics make the game more immersive—for what giant spider could possibly be scarier than the one you imagine?—but for beginners it is, to say the least, a deterrent. Just interpreting the information that's pre-sented on the screen demands a lot of study, and it's not a wild guess that most people who download *Dwarf Fortress* give up after only a couple of minutes.

But the simple graphics are not there just to scare off all but the most devoted players. They also give the game's developer time to focus on other things. Great game play and interesting mechanics are always more important than good-looking graphics, maintains *Dwarf Fortress*'s creator, Tarn Adams. It's also the reason he has spent several years adjusting and tweaking the balance in *Dwarf Fortress* and the nearly infinite number of situa-tions that can arise from the combinations of thousands of different objects, creatures, and occurrences. For the person who takes the time to understand the game's mysteries, it becomes a world that's almost got a life of its own. In an interview with the *New York Times*, Adams tells of his surprise when he discovered that the carp he programmed into the game also turned out to be danger-ous monsters with an appetite for dwarf warriors:

"We'd written them as carnivorous and roughly the same size as dwarves, so that just happened, and it was great."

Judging by the popularity of the game—*Dwarf Fortress* has been downloaded more than a million times—many agree.

Secondly, *Dwarf Fortress* is a game that is almost completely open ended. Or rather, the game ends when the player dies, which happens often in the cruel, underground world of dwarves. Other than that, the player decides what to build and how. The game puts a bunch of happy dwarves, tools, and opportunities on the table and waves good-bye with one simple request: have fun. The rest is up to the player.

Markus had quit his secure job at Midasplayer to do just that. Have fun. He loved the indie scene that had sprung up in the gaming world. While it was hard for him to put his finger on exactly what it was that attracted him, he felt at home there, much more so than as a developer with one of the industry's large, established studios, that much he knew.

His favorite online hangout was the game forum TIGSource, a meeting place for indie developers, where Markus (known as Notch in that context) quickly found a group of friends and acquaintances to talk games with. He loved the burning creativity of the indie scene, its focus on new, interesting gaming concepts rather than on elaborate graphics and expensive manuscripts. He liked that each programmer controlled his own projects entirely.

An outside observer who saw his career at this time would probably shake their head. Markus, who had dreamt of being a game developer since childhood, had had the privilege of working at two of Sweden's most successful game companies. Avalanche developed Hollywood-like productions, with nearly unlimited budgets. Midasplayer was in the forefront of development and experimented vigorously with the new potential of the web. Still, Markus had hated them both so much that he quit. What was it that rubbed him the wrong way?

Maybe it was more than just getting free of the boss who told him what to do day in and day out. "Indie" literally means independent, that an individual can develop a game without a large company doling out commissions. Markus's own interpretation of the concept is slightly different. He feels that indie is a matter of self-image. It's about creating games for their own sake, where the goal isn't to make money but to make the best game possible.

In many ways, that is a more telling definition. Except for some incredible exceptions, the gaming industry differs from other creative businesses in that the foremost game designers are seldom recognized for their work in the way famous musicians or film directors are. In the gaming world, it's the publishers or studios that are recognized after a well-received game release, seldom the individuals. That's because game development is, in most cases, a collective achievement. In a project with several hundred programmers, it's almost impossible to point out just one person as the brain or the visionary behind the whole thing. In the indie scene, on the other hand, a single programmer can put together a game of his or her own and stand behind everything from the basic vision to the implementation. You could say that the indie scene, being closer to artistry than it is to systems development, has, for the first time, given the individual game developer an identity to embrace. Markus has never thought of himself as a Java programmer, graphic artist, or musician. He sees himself as a game maker, plain and simple. The indie scene was the only place where he could be just that.

While working in web development at Jalbum, Markus resigned himself to the fact that his monthly paycheck wouldn't be coming from developing games, but it was still better to work on something else during the day in order to be able to invest his evenings and weekends in his own projects. Initially, he had seen Jalbum mostly as his ticket out of Midasplayer. Now, a couple of weeks later, he was actually enjoying it. He had developed a friendly acquaintance with Carl Manneh, the CEO. Markus recalls that his first impression of Manneh was that of a typical businessman, and though Markus wasn't the least bit interested in business, Carl Manneh's enthusiasm was impressive. He was young, quick thinking, and had already, at barely thirty years old, run three companies. The first one sold shoelaces, the second was a recording studio in central Stockholm. The third was Jalbum.

And he ran the company really well, in Markus's opinion. Carl was an entrepreneurial soul with a good head for the business logic of the Internet. Besides that, he understood Markus's ambition to develop games. He was even interested, asking questions about projects and offering some of his own thoughts. Carl stood for something completely different from what the old bosses at Midasplayer had. He encouraged Markus and made sure that he had the time and the opportunity to balance his job with what he really wanted to do.

Besides *Dwarf Fortress*, there were two other games that fascinated Markus at that time: *RollerCoaster Tycoon* and *Dungeon Keeper*. *RollerCoaster Tycoon* is an amusement-park simulator, where the player builds roller coasters; *Dungeon Keeper* is a strategy game, where the player digs cave passages and populates them with monsters and ingenious traps as protection against plundering explorers.

In *RollerCoaster Tycoon*, Markus liked the ability to build, quickly and easily, original, impressive constructions. He could spend hours dreaming up complicated roller coasters, and he wanted to engender that same creativity in his own project. *Dungeon Keepers'* contribution had mainly to do with atmosphere. Fantasy-type, torch-lit catacombs are just as much a cliché in the game world as are space battles and dwarf warriors, but it was still an environment that Markus loved. Few games had captured the nerve-tingling sensation of exploring dark, spooky caves and dungeons as well as Bullfrog's classic strategy game from 1997, in his opinion. From *Dwarf Fortress*, he wanted to bring the exciting feeling of depth and life that Tarn Adams's cult game was so good at conveying. His own game would feel more like a world to explore and to try to survive in than a narrative, segmented into ready-made challenges.

Then there was *Wurm Online* of course. The similarities between *Minecraft* and the game Markus designed with Rolf Jansson a couple of years earlier are unmistakable. In both, the player has almost complete freedom to alter the world according to his or her own whim. Like *Minecraft*, there are few built-in tasks or challenges to undertake in *Wurm Online*. The player is expected to create his or her own goals for the game alone or, if so desired, in collaboration with others.

In the spring of 2007, Markus dropped out of *Wurm Online*. Rolf had moved from Stockholm to Motala a few years earlier, the two were seeing less of each other, and

Markus knew that the big decisions about the game's development were increasingly in Rolf's hands. Besides, his Midasplayer job kept him busy.

Rolf was disappointed. *Wurm Online* had just begun to pull in enough money to give him a decent full-time salary. The sudden resignation of one of the game's founders, the friend with whom he'd worked for more than three years, was a huge blow. Initially, Markus had a bad conscience about it—it was hard not to feel like he had left his old friend in the lurch. He retained a small part of his ownership in the shared company, but turned over the rest to Rolf. A Band-Aid on the sore if nothing else, he thought.

But now, in front of the computer with *Dwarf Fortress* on the screen, Markus's thoughts were fully focused on the next project—on amusement parks, medieval catacombs, and dwarf warriors, that is to say. All that remained was to put together something new and entertaining.

At first, Markus sketched a game world that was, like many other strategy games, viewed from above. In Markus's game, the building and exploring would occur in a three-dimensional world a good deal more inviting and easy to understand than that of *Dwarf Fortress*. But the player would still control the action like an omnipotent god with a mouse, rather than seeing the world from the perspective of one's avatar.

That changed a couple of days later. Like most evenings after work, Markus was on the computer when he stumbled upon an indie game he hadn't tried before. It was called *Infiniminer*. Markus downloaded the game, installed and clicked it into motion, and then almost fell off his chair. "Oh my God," he thought. "This is genius."

Like *Minecraft*, *Infiniminer* involves digging and building. The game is enacted in square, blocky worlds automatically generated before each play. Every individual block can be picked loose from the environment and assembled into something new. Certain blocks, often the ones deep in the ground, contain rare minerals. Others are just dirt and rock to be dug through in the search for treasure.

Recognize it? No surprise there. For anyone who has played *Minecraft*, the first encounter with *Infiniminer* is eerily familiar. The game was developed by American programmer Zachary Barth, and was released in late April 2009, just weeks before *Minecraft* saw the light of day. The two games' graphics are nearly identical. There are brown dirt blocks, gray stone, and orange, bubbling lava that runs slowly over the ground.

Infiniminer was originally intended as a multiplayer game, with different teams competing to collect the most precious minerals in the shortest time. Buildings were used as a way of sabotaging the competitors' progress. But eventually players discovered that building was more fun than competing for points and they began to spend their time creating houses, castles, and other structures instead. *Infiniminer* quickly developed a devoted following, which included Markus, and in the spring of 2009, most signs pointed to Zachary Barth's game being on its way to a breakthrough. But it didn't get there, because of a particularly unhappy turn of events.

Barely a month after *Infiniminer* was released, the game's source code was leaked onto the Internet. This meant that anyone with enough programming skills could make changes to the game, and soon, innumerable downloadable copies and variations of *Infiniminer* began cropping up. For Zachary Barth, the problem was not economic—he had never hoped to make a ton of money from *Infiniminer*—it was that he lost control of how his game developed. Each of the variations of *Infiniminer* circulating on the Internet had small, incompatible differences. Two players with different versions installed could never be sure that they would be able to play with each other. Zachary Barth's plans of building a large and living multiplayer community around *Infiniminer* became impossible. The American programmer made the best of the situation and released *Infiniminer* as open source code, and gave his blessing to the game's fans to continue developing it as they wished.

After Markus became familiar with *Infiniminer*, he immediately sat down and began recoding his own game. He changed the third-person perspective to a first-person point of view and redid the graphics to make them even more blockish. It was a step away from the traditional strategy game he'd picked from his models and toward a more adventure-oriented setup. After a couple of days of frantic coding, Markus leaned back in his chair, satisfied as he saw the puzzle pieces beginning to fall into place. Building, digging, and exploring took on a totally new dimension when players saw the world through the eyes of their avatars.

In early May 2009, Markus uploaded a video recording of a very early version of *Minecraft* on YouTube. It didn't look like much more than a half-finished system for generating worlds and Markus gleefully jumping around inside it, but still, the essence of it hinted at how the game might look when it was done.

"This is a very early test of an *Infiniminer* clone I'm working on. It will have more resource management and materials, if I ever get around to finishing it," is Markus's description of the clip.

Someone on the fringes might regard what Markus did as intellectual-property theft. Without beating around the bush, he revealed where he found his inspiration and even went as far as to call *Minecraft* a clone of an existing game. But game developers, more than other kinds of artists, often find their starting point in an existing idea that they then work on, change, and polish. All studios, large and small, keep tabs on what their competitors are doing and frequently borrow from their games. Still, game developers seldom accuse others of plagiarizing. Almost all platform games originate from the mechanics that Nintendo put in place in the first *Super Mario Bros.*, released in 1985. And more or less all role-playing games build on the structure that was developed in games such as *The Bard's Tale.* That's why Zachary Barth refuses to single out Markus as a thief. He even speaks about how he himself used *Team Fortress 2* and the indie game *Motherload* as inspiration for *Infiniminer.* Actually, he's tired of the constant questions about if he feels ripped off considering the millions of players and dollars that *Minecraft* has pulled in.

"The act of borrowing ideas is integral to the creative process. There are games that came before *Infiniminer* and there are games that will come after *Minecraft.* That's how it works," says Barth.

About this time Markus, after discussing the matter with some friends at the TIGSource forum, decided to call his game *Minecraft.* The name was a combination of the words *mine*, for mining ore in shafts, and *craft*, as in building or creating something. The name is also a wink at Blizzard's strategy games *Warcraft* and *StarCraft*, and the enormously successful online role-playing game *World of Warcraft.* Initially, the game had the subtitle *Order of the Stone*, a reference to the online series *Order of the Stick*, of which Markus was a fan, but that idea was scrapped before the game was released to the public.

Markus was convinced that he was onto something big, but convincing the world around him of the excellence of his game was not so easy. A bunch of different ideas merged into *Minecraft*, and explaining them without any kind of demonstration was complicated. Over coffee with his mom, Markus attempted to describe in sweeping gestures the new project he was working on. He told her about the building, the exploration, and the atmosphere, and then explained how the game would be both easily accessible and complicated at the same time. Maybe it could develop into something great, he thought aloud. Maybe he should give notice at work and focus entirely on *Minecraft*. Ritva smiled slightly. It sounded like a really good idea, she'd said to her son. But maybe he should start by working only part-time? It wasn't entirely easy to support oneself on game development alone. He'd said that himself before.

In truth, Markus's idea was all Greek to her. Plus she remembered the year after high school, when he didn't look for work, didn't study, and barely went outdoors for days at a time. What would happen if he became just as obsessed with another project, something that could be just as important to him as building with LEGO pieces had been when he was in elementary school but that earned him next to nothing? She was worried, and yet, she saw how his eyes lit up when he talked about the game. He became confident, self-assured.

Elin better understood what Markus was thinking. She was among the first in the world to try out a working version of *Minecraft*. As soon as it was ready, Markus sent it to Elin and asked her to play. When she logged in and started up the world, what she got was basically a tech demo—a world of blocks beneath a blue sky. But Markus's intentions were immediately evident to her. A couple of minutes of digging and building and she was entrenched in the game.

"This is SO much fun!" she said to her boyfriend.

From that moment on, Elin was Markus's game tester. Every time he added a new feature to *Minecraft*, he sent her the latest version. Markus often stood watching over Elin's shoulder while she played, listening intently to her comments. If Elin liked something he'd done, he seemed to reason, the rest of the world would probably like it, too.

Even before *Minecraft* was shown to the public, Markus had made a couple of important decisions that would have a huge influence on the game's continued development. First, he wanted to document the development openly and in continuous dialogue with players, both his semiprofessional colleagues at TIGSource and any others who might be interested. Markus updated his blog often with information about changes in *Minecraft* and his thoughts about the game's future. He invited everyone who played the game to give him comments and suggestions for improvements. In addition to that, he released updates, in accordance with the Swedish saying "often rather than good" (meaning someone who prefers spontaneity over perfection). As soon as a new function or bug-fix was in place, he made it available via his site, asking players for help in testing and improving it.

Second, Markus knew from the beginning that he eventually wanted people to pay for *Minecraft*. In the back of his mind were his talks with Jakob at Midasplayer and their dream of starting their own game studio, so it seemed only natural to put a price on his game. And it was better to do it as soon as possible.

It doesn't sound very controversial, but the fact is that Markus's decision went against most of the current trends in the gaming and Internet world. Many technology prophets talk about the road to riches on the web being through charging as little as possible for your products, preferably nothing at all. At most of the well-known Internet companies, for example Google and Facebook, the cash comes mainly from ads. In the gaming industry, the trend points to "micropayments." Rovio-developed *Angry Birds*, which costs one dollar from the App Store, is maybe the best-known example. Another is the Swedish-developed online game *Battlefield Heroes*. It's a variation on the popular game that's free to play, but players can buy new equipment and better weapons for a few dollars each.

Markus disregarded all such things. *Minecraft* was to cost around thirteen dollars during the alpha phase, the first period of development, mainly because it was a sum that he felt comfortable with. When the game was completed, the price would double.

"The reason that I released the game so early was that I would never have been able to finish it otherwise. Charging money was the same thing. I knew that I would never feel that it was good enough to put a price tag on. So I charged from the start," says Markus today.

Anyone looking for more refined business logic behind what would become the most profitable gaming phenomenon of the last decade is on a fool's errand. Markus is notoriously disinterested in business and economics. When someone asks him to reveal the secret behind *Minecraft*'s unbelievable financial success, he just smiles and shrugs his shoulders. He just followed his gut, he says, did what felt right and what worked for him. To the question of what was the most important thing he learned from *Minecraft*'s early sales, Markus answers:

"I understood that an orange splash where it says 'half price' works really well. That's what I had on the site during the alpha phase."

On May 17, 2009, Markus uploaded the first playable version of *Minecraft* onto the indie forum TIGSource. "It's an alpha version, so it might crash sometimes," he warned. Other forum writers immediately began exploring the blocky world that Markus presented to them. There was a lot of digging, building, and discussing. The game crashed at times, but even at that early stage, it's clear that *Minecraft* was exerting an unusual magnetism on players.

It took just a couple of minutes for the first reactions to come. "Oh hell, that's pretty cool," someone wrote. "I hope you make something really good out of this, dude, I think it has a lot of potential," another encouraged. Barely an hour after Markus uploaded the game, the first image of a *Minecraft* construction was posted in the forum thread. "This is way too much fun. I built a bridge," wrote the person who uploaded the image. Others filled in, adding their own constructions. A castle, a fortress, a secret treasure chest. Someone wrote that he'd tried to make a boat, but the result was too ugly to make public. Someone else built a giant phallus, but never uploaded an image, just relied on a vivid description of the work: "It was such a thing of awe that Firefox decided to pack it in before I could snap a shot of that mofo."

Markus followed the postings with great interest, listening to bug reports and discussing *Minecraft*'s future with others on the forum. Friends and family remember how he told them enthusiastically about the warm welcome *Minecraft* had received. Many games are uploaded on TIGSource every day, but few struck a chord with the audience the way Markus's game had. In his head, a ray of hope began to shine. Maybe he was on the right track this time.

In early June, Markus described his intended pricing model on his blog. Those who paid for the game were promised access to all future updates at no extra cost. A free edition of *Minecraft* would still be available, but only the current half-finished version of the game. For those who bought a copy of *Minecraft* immediately, there was a discount. When the game entered beta-development, the price would be raised to $20, and the finished version would cost $26. On June 12, Markus opened for orders. Twenty-four hours later, he clicked on the sales statistics and could hardly believe his eyes. Fifteen people had paid for the game. In just twenty-four hours, more than $150 had landed in his PayPal account.

Elin and Jakob were two people who really noticed the effect the early sales successes had on Markus. Elin remembers how he obsessively followed the growing numbers of games sold. She hesitates to describe him as nervous, but clearly Markus was very focused on the early reactions to the game. Seven games purchased per day felt unbelievable.

Initially, Markus dismissed these sales as a passing fad. But every day the number of discussion threads about *Minecraft* on the game developer forum grew larger, and increasing numbers of people visited them. All the while, the sales counter continued ticking upward, slowly at first, then faster. At home in Sollentuna, Markus did a quick calculation: *If I can sell more than twenty games a day, that's enough for something approaching a decent salary*, he thought, and made up his mind. *Then I'll quit my day job. Then I'm really doing this.*

CHAPTER 8

THE HEDONIC HOT SPOT OF THE BRAIN

EARLY COMMENTS ON the first version of *Minecraft* didn't seem particularly noteworthy at the time. Reading them now, they seem rather prophetic. *Minecraft* was then a very simple game, with only a fraction of the features that it has today. You could only dig up blocks and put them where you chose; that was it. Markus hadn't had time to put in the animals, monsters, or anything else he had planned for the game. Still, the response was overwhelmingly positive. Players built things, took immediate screenshots of their creations, and uploaded them online. Within a few years, millions of others would be doing exactly the same thing. The question is why? What made *Minecraft* so easy to like right from the start?

Understanding why certain games are fun and others are not spans disciplines such as psychology, art history, and neurology. Game publishers invest enormous sums to determine what it is that will get players to spend an extra hour in front of the screen.

Minecraft completely disregards the fact that other game developers go to great lengths to create worlds in which every detail is shaped with millimeter precision. In the racing game *Gran Turismo 5*, players can whiz around the Nürburgring in an almost photo-realistically re-created Lamborghini or Ferrari racecar. The action-adventure game *Assassin's Creed II* lets the player climb tall buildings with soft, lithe movements, perfectly adapted to the jutting edges and window ledges that are there to grab hold of. Once on top of a church bell tower in fifteenth-century Florence, he or she can gaze out over an exquisitely rendered version of the city.

Does all this mean that these games are approaching reality? Not at all. A resemblance to reality in games is not only difficult to achieve, it often ruins the experience. For most players, driving a sports car along Germany's most famous racetrack needs to be much simpler than in reality. In the same manner, Ezio, the main character in *Assassin's Creed II*, must have superhuman climbing skills if the game is to be any fun. However, it's not enough that games make reality easier; in some cases they have to make it *un*real in order to retain players' interest.

In the first-person shooter game *Halo*, there are two ways you can injure enemies with a handgun: you can either shoot your opponent or, if you get close enough, you can club him with the butt of your gun. If Bungie, the company that develops *Halo*, had attempted to emulate reality, a smack of the butt would hardly cause injury at all, while a couple of gunshots would kill. In fact, the opposite is true. In *Halo*, a melee attack is often much more damaging than a gunshot. Making the game "realistic" would have made it feel one-dimensional. The design would have felt, strangely enough, illogical, since it's more difficult to get close to an enemy than to shoot one from a distance.

This is where the strange logic of games becomes evident. The point is not to emulate reality but to adapt reality to clear, functioning rules. This phenomenon is a great deal older than computer games. Take chess, where the rook is more agile than the king, and pawns can only attack diagonally. Rock-Paper-Scissors is another example—a rock bashing scissors may be plausible; the scissors cutting paper also. But paper covering the rock would probably not be regarded as a victory if it weren't necessary for the game to function.

So it's not a problem that the world that greets

Minecraft players doesn't resemble reality. Instead, the blocky graphics activate an important mental ability. The human brain is skilled at reading patterns and is especially good at finding familiar shapes like faces and human figures. That's the reason why we can see shapes in clouds and the face of Jesus on a slice of toast. When the image of a face consists of only a few lines, we fill in the missing pieces. Something similar happens in *Minecraft*. The pigs in the game resemble pink shoeboxes with heads and legs more than anything else, but there is no doubt to the player that they are pigs. Perhaps we should call the graphics "abstract" rather than simple. It's an odd fact that game graphics risk seeming more unreal the closer they approach reality. Low-resolution game characters, such as Pac-Man, the pill-eating sphere from 1980, cannot be misinterpreted. It is often easier to identify with abstract, hand-drawn figures than it is with those that almost perfectly resemble humans but don't quite hit the mark. Both robots and animated game characters often fall into that trap.

In 1970, the Japanese robotics professor Masahiro Mori coined the expression "uncanny valley." The phenomenon can be observed when you draw a diagram of how attractive or pleasing a robot or animated figure is perceived to be by a viewer. Masahiro Mori succeeded in showing that we find such figures more pleasing to look at the more they resemble humans, but only to a certain limit. Virtual human faces that come close to the real thing but lack that little extra something—life in the eyes, perhaps, or natural muscle movements—become almost repulsive to look at. They feel dead, zombielike. The recognition curve drops into a deep chasm; that's the uncanny valley. But then when the simulated face reaches an almost perfect level of detail, a level that few, if any, computer games attain today, the recognition curve turns upward again.

The characters in *Minecraft* are a comfortable distance from the uncanny valley. Playing on a server with others, a player sees fellow players as blocky figures, leaving it to each player's imagination to "animate" the characters with real personality traits. If you know your best friend is the one who is maneuvering the figure on the screen, that's who you will see. There is no preprocessed face interfering.

While *Minecraft* breaks with the gaming industry's evolution toward photo-realism, the internal logic is infallible. This becomes most obvious when you build tools from minerals you've dug up. There are many recipes hidden inside the game; for example, two parts wood and three parts stone make a pickaxe if they are put in the correct places on a grid. Change the pattern and swords, furnaces, buckets, compasses, or pretty much anything appears. But the player never receives any help with the recipes—you have to figure out for yourself how to do it, or you have to go read about it on the web. There are so many recipes and they follow such a logic that the system almost feels organic. *Minecraft* exemplifies what is meant by a game having its own universe, with its own laws and logic. It has nothing to do with reality, but everything to do with a coherent, consistent set of rules.

As with all effort in gaming, even creating a tool must lead to some reward. It's usually that the tool makes it easier to do something else, like digging up even more blocks. And pickaxes crafted from rare materials are, naturally, more effective than common ones.

Here's where the question arises of what "reward" really means in a game context. Rewards can manifest themselves in many ways: getting to see the continuation of a story, one's avatar receiving more power, getting to see a visually impressive film sequence, hearing a beautiful sound. The history of games is full of classic examples, like the *ting* you hear when Mario picks up a coin. But more than anything, the rewards are about that feeling of having solved a problem or puzzle. Why do we like that? There are theories that take us a good way down the road to an answer.

Mihaly Csikszentmihalyi is a Hungarian-American psychology professor who is interested in what it means to "feel good." So much that he has established a branch of psychology that studies happiness, contentment, and creativity. In the 1970s, he began working on a theory for a psychological state he thought he observed people sometimes attaining. He coined the concept of "flow" to describe the feeling of introverted ecstasy that successful musicians, artists, and athletes sometimes experience.

"Flow" happens when you disappear into the task you have taken on and completing it becomes your sole purpose. The basis for Csikszentmihalyi's hypothesis was laid down long before computers or video games hit the mainstream market, but in nearly every way, the condition is consistent with what players experience when they are deeply absorbed in a game. The world disappears and their hands seem to move independently as they steer their avatar toward new challenges. Good games give us challenges that are exactly the right degree of difficult. They give instant feedback and tell us if we have passed the test or not (for example, if an opponent died, or not). There are often hints to help the player along the way. Here is the essence of attaining flow; succeeding at task after task, with exactly as much resistance as we need to neither get bored because it's too easy, nor so frustrated at its difficulty that we give up.

Also, playing games does not require us to get off the couch, carry anything heavy, or expose ourselves to unpleasant weather. Instead, we effortlessly steer an alter ego through a strange, exceptional world. Each separate action—digging up a block in *Minecraft*, climbing up a building in *Assassin's Creed II*, or firing a shot in *Battlefield 3*—is accompanied by sounds and visuals that make the experience enjoyable, even when we fail. Playing the game is, in the words of the Hungarian-American psychologist, rewarding in its own right.

Perhaps this is how we must understand the balance between challenge and reward in computer games. Exactly what the reward consists of is not important, as long as the task of getting it challenges the player at exactly the right level. Perhaps our brains are simply made to enjoy succeeding at challenging things.

So, how well does this model fit *Minecraft*? In one aspect, it seems to be way off target—Markus's game doesn't have what Csikszentmihalyi says is a condition for flow: clear direction. Instead, the player invents his or her own aim—for example, building a fortress or finding a rare mineral. From this perspective, it's also obvious why some players stop playing *Minecraft* immediately; they are the ones who never get around to building anything, and therefore can't create a meaningful goal for themselves. So Csikszentmihalyi's model actually suits *Minecraft* like a glove, as long as the player makes a decision about what to aim for in the game.

If games are so suitable for putting us into a state of flow, why isn't everyone attracted to them? Are there differences in the brains of gamers? Simone Kühn believes so. She is a researcher in experimental psychology at the University in Ghent, Belgium, and is also interested in the brain's capacity to experience pleasure. Deep inside our heads, at around eye level and halfway behind the neck, there is an area of the brain called the ventral striatum. The ventral striatum can be considered our center of hedonism, the part of the brain that is activated when we enjoy or anticipate enjoying something. Food, sex, and drugs get the striatum spinning, and it is often mentioned when discussing drug abuse or people who've developed a pathological dependency on gambling. However, the striatum doesn't just turn us into slobbering hedonists; it is also connected to fast decision-making and the ability to take action. The same part of the brain that makes us attracted to fatty foods and drugs seems to help us get things done at work.

"It has been termed the hedonic hot spot of the brain. It's not often the case that a brain region is so clearly associated to one function, but with the ventral striatum it is clear that it is involved with reward processing," says Kühn.

To learn more about how playing computer games affects that place in the brain, Kühn went to Berlin. There, she found a group of test subjects and strapped helmets on them, looking into their heads with the help of an MRI device. The test subjects were asked to play an academically designed game. As expected, the striatum lit up when the subjects became involved in pushing buttons. But not everyone in equal measure. One group turned out to have larger ventral striata than others—they simply had more brain matter in this spot, especially on the left side. This group consisted of people who played computer games in their free time.

The conclusion was obvious: game players have

different brains than others. The question then becomes: What causes what? No one knows if gaming makes the striatum grow or if a congenitally larger striatum makes one more inclined to play. It's clear that certain personality traits seem to be more common among those who play a lot. They seek immediate rewards for their efforts and make decisions more quickly than others. If it could be proved that games make the brain's enjoyment center grow, then it's logical that these characteristics are strengthened by a lot of gaming. If that's the case, then gaming may make us more active and give us quicker reactions, but it might also lead us to tend to choose short-term rewards rather than working long-term toward something greater.

From Csikszentmihalyi's flow perspective, the attraction of *Minecraft* is easy to understand. It gets a little trickier when we get into Simone Kühn's research findings. *Minecraft* doesn't give the same immediate gratification as do many other games. *Minecraft* is more difficult and it only becomes really fascinating once you've spent days building a cathedral out of one-meter blocks, or digging a winding system of tunnels and furnishing it with electric rails.

Maybe that's why *Minecraft* reaches outside the usual circles of devoted gamers. One way to explain it is to see *Minecraft* as something other than a game. Perhaps graffiti or dollhouses are better comparisons. Or why not adventure travel? Nintendo's legendary game designer Shigeru Miyamoto has described something similar. He has cited his childhood in the Kansai region of Japan as the inspiration behind his classics such as *Mario Bros.*, *The Legend of Zelda*, and *Donkey Kong*. There, he would explore the countryside for hours and find his own caves and paths in the woodlands. He is also attracted to simulated danger, playing with the audience's need to experience things that make them jump but that are impossible in reality—falling from great heights or fighting colorful monsters, for example. *Minecraft* reflects a similar ambition. Few of us will ever build a cathedral of real stone, but in *Minecraft*, we can get an idea of how it feels.

The first members of the TIGSource forum who tested Markus's game discovered the same thing. They hadn't found a game; they found a playground for all they could imagine. At first, there were only a few of them. But then, as the forum threads filled up with comments praising the game and the constructions players made within it, Markus sold more and more copies of *Minecraft*. Soon, he'd discover that a lot more people than he believed possible were prepared to whip out their credit cards so they could experience it for themselves.

CHAPTER 9

"YES, YOU SHOULD PLAY THIS GAME."

JULY 2010. IT was morning as Markus logged onto his computer at home, as part of the morning routine he had developed and rather enjoyed. Every time someone bought a copy of *Minecraft*, he received an e-mail. Since most customers were in the United States, most of those e-mails came in while Markus was asleep in Sweden and when he woke up, the purchase confirmations would be waiting for him in droves. Not only had clicking through them become second nature, it put him in a great mood. To Markus, those e-mails symbolized the acknowledgement of all his hard work and bore the fruits of his labors. And so many people willing to pay for *Minecraft* was pretty good indication that things were going pretty well.

On this particular morning, four hundred e-mails were waiting in Markus's inbox. Four hundred people had bought *Minecraft* in the past twenty-four hours. Markus leaned back in his chair. He did some quick mental math. And he concluded that about $5,800 had found its way into his bank account since yesterday morning. A new record.

It had been a little over a year since the spring day when Markus first introduced *Minecraft* to the gaming world. A little over a year ago he hadn't, not in his wildest dreams, imagined that the game would make any money to speak of. For one thing, it wasn't exactly easy to get hold of. *Minecraft* wasn't available on Steam, Xbox Live Arcade, or in any of the other established online outlets. Those who wanted to try it had to somehow find their way to Minecraft.net, a simple website Markus built, then laboriously enter their credit card numbers, download the game, and install it on their own machine. Not exactly user-friendly and hardly optimal from a marketing standpoint.

But it worked anyway. As the days passed, word spread of the odd little game. The first to discover it were the already somewhat obsessed—devoted gamers and programmers looking for inspiration and the next big thing. And then word reached beyond the usual indie circles. Within a couple of months, game blogs and discussion forums started teaming with accounts from enraptured gamers showing off their creations. The more they wrote, the more eyes turned toward Markus's game. While all Markus did was continue programming and documenting his progress online.

Total sales of *Minecraft* passed twenty thousand that summer, and it was with a dizzying feeling in the pit of his stomach that Markus realized he was well on his way to becoming a rich man. He remembers to this day the happy visit to the ATM that produced the bank statement that verified he had over $150,000 (SEK 1 million) in his account. He and Elin framed the bank statement and hung it on their apartment wall. "They say that the first million is the hardest," Markus told his girlfriend with a satisfied grin.

Soon *Minecraft* caught the attention of Markus's own heroes. Brandon Reinhart, a programmer who worked on Markus's favorite game, *Team Fortress 2*, wrote on the game's blog that the next version of the game would probably be late. The development team had developed a deep and serious *Minecraft* addiction, he explained. "Yes, you should play this game," he wrote, adding a link to Markus's website. Sales more than doubled overnight.

It wasn't long before Markus was making more money from *Minecraft* than from his day job at Jalbum. He stayed on, but gradually cut back on his hours, and spent the other days at home fine-tuning *Minecraft*. Markus still believed the success was temporary. *It will be over soon*, he thought.

But sales kept climbing.

Sales were not the only thing on the up-and-up. So was Anna. After being homeless and a drug addict, after giving Markus many empty promises about cleaning up her act, Markus's sister was finally getting her life back on track. Going to rehab had led her to staying sober for several years, as did continuing to go to support groups. Now she had a new partner and a new baby daughter; a new life. For the first time since they were kids, Anna and Markus's relationship did not revolve around her dependency and did not entail her asking him for cash. And while Anna still felt guilty about their past, Markus had already put it behind them.

Even their father had been staying clean for longer stretches, and in that time Markus began to mend their relationship. He would sometimes visit Birger out at his cabin in the country, and the two of them would spend the weekend cooking, swimming, sitting together on the porch and admiring the landscape, and talking about anything and everything. Things between them were better than they'd been in years, and while his father's drug-free period would turn out to be short-lived, to say that Markus enjoyed this time of his life would be an understatement.

Markus had promised himself—even before *Minecraft*'s breakthrough—that he would, as soon as his finances allowed, dedicate himself entirely to his own gaming endeavors. He and Jakob had already invested innumerable hours in daydreaming about the game studio they hoped to create together; they already knew where the money from *Minecraft* would go: into developing *Scrolls*. Also, Markus was tired of coding alone. He needed someone to bounce ideas off of and hang out with during the day.

Giving notice at his day job was no small decision, and Markus found, to his surprise, it was more difficult to do than he'd expected. He still didn't believe his success was going to last. Sure, the money was rolling in right now. But in six months? A year? Add to that the fact that Markus had left behind his messy apartment in Sollentuna and had moved into a place with Elin in Kärrtorp. It was more important than ever to be able to count on a stable financial situation.

Jakob was facing a similarly tough decision. Unlike Markus, he had stayed on at Midasplayer, and the company continued to earn serious money. He'd been asked to step up and manage the company's game developers. For a father with a toddler at home, it was a very attractive offer. A management job with a great salary, at a company with a promising future. Jakob and Markus found themselves at the same crossroads that most people with entrepreneurial dreams encounter at some point in their lives. On the one hand: a secure work life, with a permanent job and a monthly salary. On the other hand: a rare opportunity to realize a dream. With *Minecraft* in their back pocket, they couldn't ask for better circumstances. But daring to take the next step... they would need a little shove.

That little shove came in early August 2010 in the form

of a phone call to Markus's cell phone. He answered and a polite American voice sounded on the other end. The voice introduced himself as a representative of Valve Software, congratulated Markus on *Minecraft's* success, and wondered if the Swede might be interested in visiting Valve's head office in Washington State for a cup of coffee.

To understand why Markus still gets excited when that phone call comes up, you have to appreciate the special status Valve enjoys in the gaming world. The company elicits approximately the same type of response from gamers as does Apple from gadget lovers. Valve's first hit game, *Half-Life* (from 1998) is still praised as one of gaming history's most revolutionary titles. The same goes for its sequel, *Half-Life 2*.

Valve is known mainly for two things. First and foremost, the studio's uncompromising focus on quality rather than on quantity—in its almost fifteen years of existence, Valve has only released a handful of games. There's also an unbelievably long time span between releases; *Half-Life 2* came out almost six years after part one in the series (but to be fair, honed to perfection). Valve's inordinately long gestation period has given rise to the expression "Valve time"—meaning the difference between the time that Valve promises a project will be finished and when it actually is. The next sequel in the *Half-Life* story should have been released for sales on Christmas Eve 2007. Fans are still waiting for it, patiently.

Second, Valve is an independent company, with its

founder, Gabe Newell, still at the helm as CEO. Thanks to megahits like *Half-Life*, Valve has the revenue to be able to invest in untried ideas. So for many indie developers, Valve represents the "good" side of large-scale game development: nearly inexhaustible resources to put into exactly and solely the games they choose without the influence of "the suits." Take *Portal* for example. The game was born from one developed by students at the DigiPen Institute of Technology. Valve employees caught sight of the game (*Narbacular Drop*, then) at a Careers Day at the institute. They liked it so much they offered the students jobs to develop it, and the result was one of the most talked-about and highly acclaimed game series of the first decade of the new millennium.

Markus surmised that the person on the phone was probably not interested in just a cup of coffee. He intuited two possibilities behind the polite invitation: Valve was either interested in buying *Minecraft*, or Valve was going to offer Markus a job. It's not unheard of for established game developers to take on successful indie projects, and it was possible that Valve had decided to now try to do with *Minecraft* what they'd done with *Portal* a few years earlier. But the American wouldn't say more than that Valve was impressed by *Minecraft* and would like to meet Markus and get to know him. If they could agree on the time, the American would arrange both airline tickets and hotel. Despite the elusiveness, Markus didn't need to think twice before answering yes. Job offer or no, meeting the Valve people, maybe shaking hands with Gabe Newell, that was every game developer's dream.

"Okay then," Markus agreed—he hesitated a second, then decided to go for it—"but I want first-class tickets!"

First-class tickets it was. The voice at the other end of the phone line thanked him and promised to make the arrangements as soon as possible. Markus would go visit Valve's head office the first week in September.

With the trip on the horizon, Markus and Jakob knew it would soon be time for a decision. There was no way Markus was not going. Yes, their plan to start their own studio in the fall was still the same, he told Jacob, but he still wanted to keep a foot in the door. You don't just wave off a potential job offer at Valve without some consideration.

"What would you say about moving to the United States?" he asked Elin a couple of days later.

In the time between the phone call and the ensuing Valve visit, interest in *Minecraft* grew at an astonishing rate. Markus watched in awe as the sales stats climbed to levels he'd never imagined. During one twenty-four-hour period, more than 23,000 copies sold. Almost one game every three seconds.

One day Markus received a grim e-mail from PayPal. The e-mail explained that his account had been temporarily blocked because clearly, he must be involved in some kind of criminal activity to have so much money flowing in so fast. At that time, Markus had almost $860,000 in his PayPal account. Swedish and international media outlets alike began to contact him, asking for interviews. Within a couple of months, from being one of thousands of anonymous amateur programmers, Markus had risen to the status of international gaming celebrity.

It was around this time that the signature hat debuted in Markus's life. He says he got the idea from Jakob, who showed up one day to a meeting wearing one just like it. *Looks sharp*, thought Markus, and went to find one for himself. After trying out several different styles, he chose a black fedora. A similar hat graces the head of Indiana Jones. Michael Jackson often wore one, too.

Markus says it's mostly coincidence that the hat is ever-present in his ensemble. But it can also be read as a symbol of his sudden fame. While it's not uncommon for programmers to work under an alias, few have created so definitive an alter ego as has Markus. Notch is as outspoken and boisterous as Markus is shy and taciturn. Markus likes few things less than speaking in front of a group of people, but on Twitter and his blog Notch will make X-rated puns and biting remarks to other game developers in front of an audience of hundreds of thousands. Markus seldom uploads photographs of himself on the Internet; instead he goes with the picture of Notch, a hand-drawn caricature, with a big, lavish beard and the trademark hat. Markus isn't in any way secretive about his true identity, but it's obvious that—consciously or not—he nurtures two radically different sides of his personality. One is private, withdrawn, and has thinning hair. The other is public, likes attention, and always has the hat pressed down over his ears.

Valve booked Markus at the Westin, the luxury skyscraper hotel in central Bellevue. He had a room near the top. Through the window, he could see far to the west, past the well-kept suburbs by Lake Washington to the city of Seattle beyond. Markus noted that all the luxury homes by the lakeside had pools. You could live a good life here if, if that's what you wanted. Close to the water, lots of room, for both him and Elin. It had to be expensive, but a programmer at Valve, just a short drive away, could probably afford it.

Meanwhile, things were still going undeniably well with *Minecraft*. A couple of weeks before his trip to the United States, Markus had asked on his blog if there might be some *Minecraft* players in the Seattle area who were interested in meeting up with him while he was in town. He was free all day Tuesday. Maybe they could organize something?

"It doesn't have to be anything fancy, perhaps a café somewhere. And I figured we could call it MinecraftCon 2010 even if it's just three people sitting around in uncomfortable silence for twenty minutes," he wrote.

When Markus walked into the little park in Bellevue at the appointed time, more than fifty people had found their way there. Several streamed the gathering live on the Internet via their cell phones. Some were dressed as

Minecraft characters. One young man is seen in photos from the meet wearing a full-length Creeper costume built out of green-painted cardboard. For several hours, Markus answered questions about *Minecraft* and shared his thoughts on the future of the game and his plans for the company he was thinking of starting with Jakob. The sky was overcast when the meeting came to an end, but Markus walked away smiling ear to ear.

The evening before his meeting at Valve, Jakob and Markus chatted on Skype. Jakob asked Markus what he would say if the question of employment came up, but he didn't get a straight answer.

"I want to find out what they want," was all Markus said.

Markus understood, just as his friend in Stockholm did, that there was a lot riding on the next day's meeting, for both of them. If Markus decided to stay in Seattle, their common venture would never be. If not, they vowed to make it happen.

"I'll get back to you in twenty-four hours," Markus promised.

Once the conversation had ended all Jakob could do was wait. In the back of his mind, he realized that the next day would decide his fate. He would either accept the management position at Midasplayer, which would mean more meetings, more responsibility, and less time for coding and game development, or he and his best friend would launch their dream project. The decision was entirely Markus's.

Markus remembers his visit at Valve's headquarters as a jumble of impressions. Before he was allowed into the office, he had to sign a nondisclosure agreement, promising not to tell anyone about the half-finished productions he would see in there. He met Robin Walker, the man who wrote the original *Team Fortress* and was employed by Valve to lead development of the sequel. Brandon Reinhart, who'd written the post on the *Team Fortress 2* blog that made *Minecraft* sales soar, showed Markus around. Markus did indeed get to shake hands with Gabe Newell. The Valve boss was very busy, Markus recalls, but the fact that he seemed to know of both him and *Minecraft* felt like an honor.

Afterward, Markus was shown into a conference room with a man from Valve's Human Resources department. The man spoke candidly about the corporate culture at Valve and what it was like to work for the company. Markus told him a little about himself and his plans for *Minecraft* before realizing that he was in the middle of a job interview. Valve had prepared a programming exercise. The man from the HR office—Markus doesn't remember his name—asked Markus how he would go about programming an elevator. Markus thought for a while, then answered in as much detail as he could. The Valve representative listened, nodded his head, and fired some additional questions at Markus where appropriate.

When the exercise was over, papers were put aside. The assessment: you are a gifted programmer, but you're not used to working in a group. We can help you with that. Markus listened intently when the opportunities at Valve were described to him. It was perhaps the most sought-after place of employment in the business. A chance to make a difference and to be a part of the absolute cutting edge of game development. We would like to work with you, he was told. Are you interested in working for us?

This is where the story could have taken a different turn. Markus could have said yes and moved to Seattle. Maybe he and Elin would have lived in one of the luxury homes by Lake Washington, with both a pool and a view of the lake. Maybe *Minecraft* would have become a downloadable game in Valve's Steam shop. Maybe Markus would have simply left *Minecraft* behind to work with a couple hundred other Valve programmers on the next installment in the *Half-Life* series.

But that didn't happen. Markus describes it as one of the hardest decisions of his life, but when the HR person asked him that question, Markus answered politely but firmly. No.

"Somehow, I felt that *Minecraft* was maybe my chance to create a Valve, rather than work at Valve," he says today.

On the other side of the Atlantic, Jakob sat at home in Stockholm, his cell phone in hand. It beeped. A new text message from Markus: "You can quit your job." The next morning, Jakob did just that.

CHAPTER 10

THE SQUID SITUATION

IT WAS EVENING in Stockholm, but it would be a while before the late summer sun would set. Markus, Jakob, and Carl Manneh, Markus's former boss as Jalbum, sat at a table at Ljunggrens Restaurant, on Götgatan. A server glided up to the table and they ordered sashimi. The subject at hand was starting a company.

A few days had passed since Markus had returned from his visit to Valve. The two friends were ready to start their company, but there were some knots that first needed to be untangled. Markus was already netting tens of thousands of dollars daily in *Minecraft* sales. Letting Jakob in as a partner in the company would mean he'd be giving away half of his creation—hundreds of thousands of dollars—with no guarantees. Markus wasn't interested in starting a company by himself, but he also didn't want to risk destroying his friendship with Jakob over money, nor did he want to be Jakob's boss. They were friends, and friends don't hire each other, they reasoned.

That's why they'd brought a business plan to the dinner table. Today, no one remembers its exact details, just that the structure of the company the two programmers described to Carl was extremely complicated. Markus and Jakob would own the company together, but not really, and somewhere, a huge loan would compensate for the financial inequality of the relationship.

Carl chewed his fish and listened. For him, the evening was also something of a job interview. Shortly before, after leaving Jalbum to work full-time with *Minecraft*, Markus had carefully asked if Carl knew of anyone who would be a good CEO for the company he wanted to start. Carl Manneh had answered yes and immediately nominated himself. Now he was here, listening to two excited programmers describe a crazy idea for a company. Not that the business would have any problems staying afloat; he knew very well that *Minecraft* was already pulling in enormous sums of money. But the structure Markus and Jakob were suggesting was among the most bizarre he had ever heard of.

Carl gives a discreet impression the first time you meet him. He doesn't speak more than necessary and doesn't brag nearly as much as he could. His facial expressions seldom reveal what is really going on in his mind; you could call it a poker face, or just prudence. Regardless, it's a characteristic useful in negotiations, both with giant international companies and with gifted programmers who have strange ideas about how to run a company. When Markus and Jakob finished, Carl pushed his plate aside and volunteered, as humbly as possible, his alternative. The duo— or the three of them if he were trusted—would form a new company they owned together. Markus would keep the immaterial rights to *Minecraft* in his own company, writing a license that gave the new company exclusive rights to develop and sell the game. No one needed to give away his life's work and no one became the other's boss. The future CEO excused himself and went off to the men's room. The two programmers sat quietly at the table for a little while. Then Jakob turned to Markus.

"You know, I feel about seven years old right now."

"Yeah, I know what you mean."

It was perhaps at that moment the business structure of *Minecraft* was nailed down. Markus and Jakob already had an idea of what kind of company they wanted to start. At Mojang, everything would revolve around really great games, innovative games. They would brainstorm ideas and together develop the games they had always dreamed of. Markus wanted to work on *Minecraft* for another six months, and after that, the money would finance new projects—starting with *Scrolls*. With the millions from *Minecraft* safe in the bank, there was no reason to compromise that vision. But they needed someone to keep finances in order, to see to the financial development and all the other stuff that belongs to the world of business. Markus and Jakob had only a vague idea of how to run a company, even less of the experience necessary to steer the enormous endeavor that they'd decided to undertake. After dinner at Ljunggrens, the two programmers agreed—Carl was the right man for the job. Markus and Jakob offered him a position, a place on the board, and a partnership in the new company. Carl accepted. On September 17, 2010, Mojang AB was registered, with Markus Persson and Jakob Porser as main owners and Carl Manneh as CEO. They took the name from *mojäng*, the Swedish word for "thingamabob" or "whatchamacallit," dropping the umlaut from over the letter *a*.

With the licensing model Carl suggested, most of the money from *Minecraft* went to Markus. The sliver remaining for Mojang would still be more than enough to hire several programmers, build upon *Minecraft*, and to begin looking toward the future of the company.

First and foremost, they needed an office. They chose an apartment just a couple of blocks away from Ljunggrens, a few stories up in a building on Åsögatan—a more carefully considered location than it might seem at first glance. The blocks around Medborgarplatsen on Södermalm are, to game developers, historic ground. A short stroll through the area surrounding Mojang's office will take you by several famous game studios, where games worth millions of dollars are developed each year.

Begin at the door of Mojang, on Åsögatan, and turn west. On Götgatan, you'll find Paradox Interactive's office. Paradox is one of the world's most famous strategy-game studios and publishes titles such as *Europa Universalis* and *Hearts of Iron.* Avalanche has its studio on the other side of the same building. Around the corner, more than seventy employees work for Electronic Arts–owned Easy Studios, which develops the online game *Battlefield Heroes.* Stop for a second and turn southward. On the horizon, less than a mile away, just over the Skanstull Bridge, you can just see the sports arena Globen. Next to the giant sphere is the site of the infamous police raid on the file-sharing site Pirate Bay in 2006. The game studio Fatshark is also located there, perhaps best known for the role-playing game *Krater,* which takes place in a postapocalyptic Karlstad (a city in Swedish Värmland). Continue north on Götgatan, past the skateboard ramps at Medborgarplatsen. At Slussen, you can peek up toward the Glass House by the dock, where DICE is enthroned in its headquarters.

This is where most Stockholmers get on the subway. A visitor interested in the Internet can instead walk up Katarinavägen to Renstiernas gata were, in an old bunker

Markus Persson, Jakob Porser, and Daniel Kaplan at work in the Mojang office. Photo by Elin Zetterstrand.

under Mariaberget, there is a data center belonging to the Internet company Bahnhof, the former home of the world-famous whistleblower site Wikileaks. If you then turn north, walk through Gamla stan and past Kungsträdgården, you'll arrive at Birger Jarlsgatan and the headquarters of the music company Spotify.

Stockholm is a small city, but per capita, few cities in the world have meant more for the development of IT. If you ask anyone you meet in Stockholm what he or she does for a living, the answer probably has something to do with computers. The fact is that systems developers make up the largest single occupational category in the city; there are more professionally active programmers in Stockholm than there are nurses' aides, salespeople, or economists.

For the past three years the international business school INSEAD has ranked Sweden as the world's second most innovative country—after Switzerland, but ahead of Hong Kong, Singapore, and the United States. Today, Sweden is also one of the world's most broadband-dense countries, with nearly 100 percent coverage, calculated by population. Besides great broadband connections, large investments have made it possible for Swedish IT companies to grow. It's easy to get stuck harping on the many bankruptcies of the early twenty-first century, but many venture capitalists have also made a lot of money on fast-growing Swedish technology firms. For example, those who invested in Spotify in 2008 watched as the value tripled in only two years. Companies such as Skype, Tradera, and MySQL have also pulled in big money for their investors. In these contexts Scandinavia is significantly overrepresented, being home to 22 percent of Europe's largest software companies despite accounting for only a few percent of Europe's population. In the last few years, one tenth of all sales ("exits" in investor-speak), for a total of more than a billion dollars, have been made in the Scandinavian countries.

The question is, why has it turned out that way? Some people point to a straightforward and uncomplicated business culture. Paradoxically, others credit it to Sweden's small population. Just over 9 million residents are just not enough to sustain a company selling only to the domestic market. Another country with similar challenges is Israel, which also has a small population and has made large technological advances. Both Israeli and Swedish technology companies are forced from the beginning to think globally and aim for the world market. That same logic applies to the game industry. Apart from a few successes with games built around well-known children's-book characters, such as Mulle Meck (Gary Gadget) and Pettson and Findus, Swedish game developers have always worked with an international audience in mind. That's why they could make early contacts with international publishers and learn the economic structure of the global game industry.

However, just as important for the growth of the Swedish gaming industry has been the fact that Sweden consumes the pop-culture diet of the English-speaking world. That's what Per Strömbäck, spokesperson for the Swedish game industry's interest group Dataspelsbranschen says.

"We discovered *Dungeons and Dragons* at the same time as the Americans did. We've read the same comics and listened to the same music," he explains.

That, combined with a good command of English from an early age, has given Swedish developers an advantage in the art of creating games with the right cultural content to reach an international audience.

"It's given us an enormous edge in comparison to many other countries in Europe. They have the technical knowledge, but their cultural frames of reference have been totally different," says Per Strömbäck.

From the perspective of the gaming industry, the IT bubble—and especially its collapse early in the first decade of the twenty-first century—was of great significance. Large numbers of newly started IT companies, which only a couple of years earlier had been hyped to the heavens, crashed spectacularly. The immediate result was that tens of thousands of experienced programmers were thrown out of work. Given the well-developed digital infrastructure in Sweden, this created very fertile breeding ground for technology entrepreneurs, as well as a nearly bottomless labor pool for game-development companies to dip into.

Mojang's office on Södermalm may have been right smack dab in the middle of the city's game cluster, but from the street there were no visible signs that the building now harbored one of the world's most talked-about game studios. To enter, visitors had to press a button on the intercom marked with a small, discreet sign that read "Mojang." Most of the time it didn't work. The intercom was hooked up wrong and was connected to some other phone somewhere in the building (no one ever succeeded in figuring out exactly which one). If you didn't have Markus's, Carl's, or Jakob's telephone number, you had to press another button instead and ask one of the neighbors to open the front door.

With time, the shabby apartment became a little cozier. One of the walls was covered in artificial grass and decorated with a large Mojang logo lit from behind. The entire back wall was decked out with a painting of mine shafts and small figures inspired by *Minecraft's* blocky graphics. The office soon felt typical of a young company in a creative business, equal parts playground and workplace. Anyone who'd worked for a quickly-growing dot-com startup during the late nineties would have felt at home.

It took Carl a few months to extract himself from his

job at Jalbum, which he'd had for two years. But it's not surprising that he accepted Markus and Jakob's offer. In 2010, Jalbum posted a loss of over $570,000, and this with a turnover of just over $425,000. The company had costs that more than doubled their revenues, and that was a good year. It's not unusual for new companies to show initial losses, but there's a limit, after which investors lose their patience and want their money back. It would be safe to say that Jalbum was approaching that limit when Carl decided to cut his losses and leave.

Nothing could be more different from Jalbum than Mojang. There, Carl saw the opportunity to lead a company that was starting out with an initial success. Even as Mojang was being founded, there was plenty of buzz about *Minecraft*. At Jalbum, Carl regularly had to badger his way into meetings with investors and then, once there, to more or less beg them to buy shares of the company so he could keep paying his workers' wages. Now it was the opposite. Now investors called him asking to be allowed to put cash into Mojang, but Carl didn't need them.

Paying wages was not the problem; instead, the challenge lay in finding the right people to pay. And it needed to happen fast. They needed someone to take care of the server that players logged into so that Markus could devote his energy to the game. The website where people bought the game was due for an overhaul, and someone needed to get started on a version of *Minecraft* for smartphones. Carl, Jakob, and Markus made recruitment a high priority, and in less than a year, Mojang went from being a small startup to being a miniature gaming empire. Of the handful of new hires, everyone, except Carl Manneh and Daniel Kaplan who were brought on as business developers, was either a programmer or a graphic designer.

One of the first to be hired was Jens Bergensten, a tall, skinny programmer with long red hair in a ponytail. Markus had met him the year before at No More Sweden.

"Markus was already somewhat of a local hero by then. *Minecraft* had been around for a couple of months, and everyone knew it was his game," says Jens.

When the two met for the first time at No More Sweden, Jens had just begun playing *Minecraft*. He'd brought a friend, Pontus Hammarberg, and a severe case of the flu.

"Pontus had just returned from the United States and had probably brought the swine flu back. We sat up around-the-clock playing *Minecraft*. When I slept, I dreamt fever dreams about how my buildings fell apart. They were large pyramids crashing down, and I was forced to fix them," he says.

Like Markus, Jens's interest in programming games has followed him since childhood. When he was twelve, he got fed up with the fact that only two people could play at a time in the 1980s game *Nibbles*, a variant of the classic cellphone game *Snake*. By fooling around with the code, he found exactly which parts needed to be copied in order to let three people play the game simultaneously. Along with that find, Jens also discovered a fascination for programming. He understood that all those rows of incomprehensible combinations of symbols made up the game itself. Games were fun, he thought, so obviously code was also going to be fun. After finishing school, he worked as an IT consultant for a while, then later became one of several programmers to work on the Swedish web game *Planeto*. He wrote his own games in his free time, participated in contests, and socialized with other programmers.

"I'm not the world's best programmer. I just happen to work very well with Markus. We have the same design philosophy and the same sources of inspiration," says Jens.

Officially, Mojang hired Jens to program the server parts of *Scrolls*. But *Scrolls* was mostly just an idea in Jakob's head when Jens started working on it, so he asked if he could sit down and check out the code behind *Minecraft* instead. The next version of the game was to be released before Christmas. To finish it on time, Markus accepted all the help he could get, and better yet from someone who, like himself, had dreamed of making a living developing games since he was a kid.

Once installed at Mojang, Jens tried to get a handle on the code that Markus had written, which might sound like a cakewalk for someone who has never done programming. But writing code is creating art. Give the same problem to two programmers and they'll give you two completely different solutions. And few will come up with constructions as odd as Markus's. He's a lone inventor—a solo programmer, through and through. Wrapping one's head around his creation entails, in a way, understanding how his brain works. And it's a brain that has earned him membership in Mensa.

As the end of 2010 was approaching, Markus and the others took some time off for Christmas. Jens, who doesn't like Christmas, went to work as usual. The office was empty, most of the nearby lunch restaurants were closed for the holidays, and the heating system in the turn-of-the-previous-century building was broken. It was below freezing outside and pretty cold inside the office too. Wearing his jacket and scarf, Jens sat there alone and continued working on *Minecraft*, having been given no instructions except to try "to build a few features," as Markus had told him in passing before taking off for the holidays.

He spent a lot of time on wool. On dyeing it, especially. Jens liked the square-shaped sheep that scampered around in the *Minecraft* world, but thought that their color was boring. If players could only get some more colors, then they would have yet another way to modify their environment, he figured. He used his frozen fingers to type out different ways of extracting dyes from minerals. He pondered the color black for a long time and came to the conclusion that squids would be the natural source from which it could be extracted in the *Minecraft* world. And so he created an appropriately blocky squid figure and programmed it into the game. A few days after the New Year, it was time to demonstrate his creations.

Carl stood nervously, shifting his weight from side to side as Jens clicked the new animals onto the screen. Markus stood next to him. Carl knew that there was a very real possibility that the creator of the game they all made a living on would hit the brakes and reject all of it. A real possibility of instigating a conflict that could put a big stick in the spokes of the company wheels. An exaggeration? Not at all. No one had ever touched Markus's life work before. If you take game development as seriously as he does, the situation could be compared to Michelangelo's apprentice having worked overtime one weekend painting his own people on the ceiling of the Sistine Chapel. *Shit, meet fan*, Carl thought.

However, when Jens demonstrated his new features on screen, Markus's lips parted in a smile. Here was someone who got it. Now and then, he asked a question, and Jens patiently answered. After that session, it was obvious that Jens would receive an entirely overhauled job description. Now there were two people developing and designing *Minecraft*.

CHAPTER 11

A DILEMMA CONCERNING HOUSE CATS

"I'M GOING TO demonstrate to you how I really don't play *Minecraft* like other people," says the voice on the YouTube film.

The viewer peers into what looks like a deep shaft. The walls are gray and are built out of bedrock. The gamer, Halkun, calls it a well.

"I'm sure you're probably thinking, 'Why, Halkun, that is a very, very deep well!' And I'm going to show you the reason why. It is currently holding. . . "

The camera turns 180 degrees.

"...this!"

A structure looms up, so large it seems to disappear into the distance. The Starship *Enterprise*. In full scale. It'll boggle the mind of anyone who has painstakingly put block to block to build something in *Minecraft*. Creating the whole spaceship from the TV show *Star Trek* must have taken weeks, maybe months.

The clip continues and Halkun gives a guided tour, talking about the model. The film has been viewed over 10 million times and is a typical example of many people's first *Minecraft* encounter.

"I haven't slept yet, so I'm gonna be a little loopy!" says Halkun triumphantly.

Minecraft's breakthrough coincided almost perfectly with the rise of the YouTube phenomenon *Let's Play*. It's exactly what it sounds like—a person recording himself or herself playing a popular computer game. The video clip often has a voice track of the player describing what's happening on the screen and talking about his or her impressions of the game. *Let's Play* is closely related to an older but similar phenomenon called *Machinima* (a combination of the words *machine* and *cinema*), a kind of film genre that uses the game world as the stage and its characters as actors. It may sound incredibly specialized, but *Machinima* has long been an established form of expression in the gaming world.

Minecraft and *Let's Play* turned out to be a good match. Since *Minecraft* encourages its players to create their own goals and challenges, each gamer's experience is unique. In the gaming world, concepts such as emergent gameplay and emergent storytelling are used to describe these phenomena. For many players, the main objective in *Minecraft* is not the game itself, but rather the documentation and public viewing of their creations.

One might assume it's a hobby for a nerdy and obsessive group of people, except that the number of people drawn to the *Minecraft* videos is staggering. In the spring of 1966, John Lennon said in an interview that the Beatles were "more popular than Jesus." Markus has never expressed himself in the same terms, but might have significantly more reason to do so. Calculated in number of Google searches, *Minecraft* briefly surpassed Jesus in popularity in early 2011. During the summer of 2010, YouTube's in-house analysts named *Minecraft* the year's fastest-growing trend. There are several million video clips about the game. During the month of May 2011 alone, more than 35,000 *Minecraft* films were uploaded—that's more than a thousand a day—and while most of them are only viewed a few times, truly popular clips can attract a huge audience. The most widely viewed *Minecraft* clip ever is "Revenge," a cover of Usher's hit song, "DJ Got Us Fallin' in Love," complete with a music video in which a *Minecraft* character sings about his hardships with thieving Creepers. Nineteen-year-old Californian Jordan Maron, more well known as "Captain Sparklez," created it. At the time of writing, "Revenge" had been viewed over 92 million times.

Two more *Minecraft* filmmakers who have attained similar levels of stardom are Simon Lane and Lewis Brindley, two young Englishmen who are collectively the heart of the *Let's Play* phenomenon The Yogscast. In about four years their YouTube channel has racked up nearly 1.8 billion views. It's not easy to describe a Yogscast clip to an outsider. Like popular TV shows, Yogscast is divided into seasons. Each episode is around twenty minutes long, and new ones are uploaded to YouTube every week or so. The setup resembles a kind of improvisational theater, with the *Minecraft* world as the stage, props, and cohesive frame of reference. Most often, Simon and Lewis follow a loosely written script with a fantasy theme, but improvise wildly and supply the characters with their own voices.

The third season of Yogscast is based on Simon and Lewis's avatars Honeydew and Xephos (one is a Tolkien-inspired dwarf warrior with a red beard, the other, a *Minecraft* version of Commander William Riker, from the TV show *Star Trek: The Next Generation*). They save the world from the evil wizard Israphel. The two men are funny, quick-witted, and likable. They often lose their train of thought, start to laugh, or get distracted from the story by something irrelevant that catches their interest. For the viewer, the experience is reminiscent of listening to two guys playing a computer game together, which is, more or less, exactly what it is.

Successful *Let's Play* filmmakers earn big money from their works. For a few years, YouTube has been sharing a slice of its massive advertising revenue with those who provide content for the site, but it's hard to find out exactly how much. Google, YouTube's owner, is very tight-lipped about what the agreements look like. Also, the revenue varies depending on the season, choice of subject, and how much ad room Google's sales department succeeds in booking at a given time. But the consensus among filmmakers is that the video ads shown before a film clip generate between one and two dollars per thousand views for the creator of the clip. It doesn't sound like a lot, but with the enormous numbers of viewers that YouTube videos attract, the dollars quickly add up. Jordan Maron is supporting himself completely on the revenue from "Revenge" and other video clips. In a good month, Simon Lane and Lewis Brindley can make tens of thousands of dollars from their Yogscast episodes.

Not everyone is lucky enough to live off of YouTube fame, but many video makers can supplement their normal income with a few hundred dollars extra a month by playing *Minecraft* for an audience. SethBling (known to the public only by his handle) is one of them. His day job is at Microsoft's Xbox division in Seattle, a job that would make many a programmer envious. On his free evenings and weekends, he invests almost all his time in playing *Minecraft*.

SethBling came into contact with *Minecraft* through a roommate. He approached the game with a programmer's eye and quickly discovered redstone. After experimenting with it for a few weeks, he decided to begin uploading videos of his creations to YouTube. On his channel, there are demonstrations of how redstone can be used to build elevators and train stations, automatic doors and a machine to teleport wolves. He has also re-created classic computer games such as *Minesweeper* and *Donkey Kong*, fully playable within the *Minecraft* world. His work consists of complex, detailed constructions that spin *Minecraft* in completely new directions, and actually have more in common with exercises in programming or engineering than with gameplay.

"I like *Minecraft* for precisely the same reason that I like programming. I have full control of the world and can shape it exactly as I choose. I can test different constructions and mechanical systems in order to see what the results are," he says.

Re-creating classic games in *Minecraft* has become something of a distinguishing mark for SethBling. His breakthrough came when Markus began taking notice of his creations, thanks to a video that was popular on the discussion forum Reddit. In it, the video maker showed how he had re-created the classic Nintendo game *Duck Hunt* in *Minecraft*. Markus found the link, had a good laugh at the clip, and tweeted it to his followers on Twitter.

In the world of *Minecraft*, being mentioned by Markus on Twitter is called being "Notched." A quick look at the *Minecraft* inventor's account gives us a clue as to why such a seemingly unpretentious action has a name of its own. At the time of writing, over 700,000 people follow Markus on Twitter. The short message, with a link to SethBling's ingenious creation, was the digital equivalent of sending a letter to almost all of central Stockholm with a promise of free entertainment in exchange for a mouse click. Within forty-eight hours, 300,000 people had seen the film. In a flash, SethBling had 4,500 new subscribers to his YouTube channel.

"Notch doesn't tweet about YouTube clips very often, but he seems to be nerdy in exactly the same way I am. That's lucky for me," says SethBling.

In a good month, he makes a couple thousand dollars from YouTube.

Markus's status as the creator of *Minecraft* gives him considerable sway in the world of the game. A single link from his Twitter account puts a spotlight on whoever has his attention, a kind of fame that can also be turned into revenue through YouTube ads. It's probably one reason that the image of Markus, in a pixely and stylized shape, recurs in many of the most impressive *Minecraft* projects you can see in films.

While Markus's status is self-evident, he is far from the only one with great influence in the world of *Minecraft*. After all, he's not the one uploading the vast number of films online—millions of players are doing that. Which means that neither Markus nor anyone else at Mojang has much control over how the image of *Minecraft* is shaped on the Internet.

Mojang has never paid a dime for ads or PR for *Minecraft*. Instead, the players themselves have generated the enormous hype surrounding the game. It's a perfect example of "viral marketing," the art of utilizing people's social networks to spread awareness about something new. The extensive YouTube community that has grown around *Minecraft* isn't just the result of the game's popularity; it's also the main cause of it being a hit from the start. Every time a *Minecraft* player uploads a video to YouTube, the chance increases that someone, somewhere will notice the game and decide to try it out. And the more people who play *Minecraft*, the more video clips are uploaded. If it hadn't been for Yogscast, Captain Sparklez, SethBling, and all the other YouTube celebrities, *Minecraft* would never have reached such a large audience as it has today.

That would be a nightmare scenario for a company with an obsessive need for control. Big companies hire hordes of PR consultants, marketers, and crisis managers to chisel out communication strategies, advertising campaigns, and rules for what information the company will divulge. All of this is thrown overboard when unbridled YouTube filmmakers are allowed to take over.

Alex Leavitt is someone who closely examines that phenomenon. He's a researcher at the University of Southern California, focused on culture, media, and digital communication, and he is interested in how the Internet affects the production of creative works and changes the way we relate to and consume popular culture. *Minecraft* is one of his primary objects of study.

"*Minecraft* is this obscure little game that became a worldwide phenomenon in more or less a couple of weeks. It just exploded. I want to understand how all these millions of people playing it have affected its development," says Leavitt.

Alex Leavitt regards *Minecraft* as an example of what he calls "open-source culture." By that he means popular culture that is created symbiotically by its originators and its users. American academic Lawrence Lessig has coined the concept "read/write culture" for more or less the same thing. Both point to a form of cultural production that preempts the traditional concepts of producer and consumer.

What makes *Minecraft* such a wonderful object of study, says Leavitt, is that the game became popular long before it was finished. As the finished version wasn't released until MineCon 2011, players, at an early stage, had the opportunity to influence how the game would look and play. For years Markus has been engaged in constant dialogue with his players about the future of *Minecraft*. On his blog he has comprehensive documentation of successes as well as mistakes and thoughts about the game's development. On Twitter and in discussion forums, he has consistently encouraged players to give him feedback for future versions. Responding to the hundreds of suggestions and opinions that pour in daily would be impossible, but Markus can often be seen on discussion threads about *Minecraft*, and he talks daily with his players on Twitter. If nothing else, he's created a feeling of accessibility; anyone can offer a suggestion and maybe have it taken into account in the next version of *Minecraft*.

Markus's constant presence also creates a strong emotional bond between the game and its players. When Carl wants to impress other CEOs and company bigwigs, he doesn't mention the millions of people worldwide who play *Minecraft*, or the five thousand people in Las Vegas who stood up and applauded when Markus got up onstage. Instead, he mentions what in marketing lingo is called "user engagement." Mojang's figures show that 75 percent of those who paid for *Minecraft* in the last two years are still active players. They are what Carl would call "monthly active users." According to him, this many of them may well be a world record. Or, as one player says, "It doesn't feel like you've bought a game. It feels like you own a part of it."

Alex Leavitt likes to talk about "narratives" in a more abstract way. In a piece of music, a book, or a more traditionally designed game, the narrative is built in. The composer has designated the melody, the game designer programs the challenges that lie on the way to the next level, the playwright has worked on the dramaturgy, and the actor interprets the role for the camera. In *Minecraft*, a meaningful narrative arises in the interplay between gamer and game.

"When you talk about movies, music, or games, the creative process typically takes place far from the user. *Minecraft* doesn't work that way. It is better seen as a platform, where the users provide the content," Leavitt says.

In Creative Mode, designed for players who just want to build without worrying about monsters, this can be taken to an extreme. For a long time, Markus was opposed to such a play mode in *Minecraft*. The whole challenge would vanish, was his reasoning. Where's the fun in that? However, among players, Creative Mode turned out to be

Markus Persson, Carl Manneh, and Jens Bergensten preparing for MineCon 2011. Photo courtesy of Mojang.

possibly the most popular style of play. Markus listened and, when the beta version of *Minecraft* was released, one of the big innovations was better support for the users who wanted to re-create things such as the Eiffel Tower in full size rather than worry about being attacked by zombies.

That decision, which originated with the players and not with Markus, is perhaps the strongest contributing factor of why *Minecraft* grew into such a phenomenon. Without Creative Mode, few of the most impressive *Minecraft* constructions would have been built—the creations that have done the most to give the game attention and attract new players.

The strong sense of commitment that *Minecraft* instills in its players is also a reason that some of the Internet world's most influential investors have taken an interest in the game. One of them, David B. Pakman, was quick to see the potential of Mojang's creation. In the 1990s, he had worked for Apple and founded the division that would later create products such as iTunes and the iPod. He has been the CEO of eMusic.com, one of the world's largest digital music stores, and for the past couple of years has been a partner in the venture capital firm Venrock Associates, which owns significant stakes in several leading Internet companies.

David Pakman discovered *Minecraft* when his kids began playing it after school. He watched, captivated, as they sat for hours in front of the computer, longer than with any other game, and he realized that the odd little creation from Sweden was something extraordinary. Pakman contacted Carl to hear more about *Minecraft* and to ask if he could offer some advice to the newly started company. Since then, he's been an informal adviser for Mojang on questions regarding business strategy and development. He has also become a devoted *Minecraft* player.

David Pakman is polite in a typically American fashion. He is careful not to criticize anything about Markus's creation or to describe *Minecraft* with anything but praise. However, on one point he is refreshingly clear: the true value in *Minecraft* is not in the game, its inventor, or anything that Markus or Mojang's programmers have done. The real value lies in the enormous community of devoted players gathering around *Minecraft* and filling it daily with new content.

Actually, David Pakman doesn't think *Minecraft* should even be referred to as a game. Markus's creation has more in common with social networks such as Facebook and Twitter, he feels. *Minecraft* is inherently a social experience. It's an activity to gather around, and therefore also a reason to socialize. If Facebook can be likened to a kind of hangout spot on the Internet, maybe a bar or a restaurant, then *Minecraft* is the digital equivalent of people meeting to play soccer together.

That point of view has serious implications for the future of *Minecraft*, and for what Markus, Jens, Jakob, and the others at Mojang spend their days working on.

There are millions of enthusiastic players out there with ideas about new functions, new monsters, challenges, and experiences to add to *Minecraft*. The developers at Mojang can't possibly compete with that. If *Minecraft* is to become as lucrative as possible, David Pakman says, it would perhaps be wise if Markus and Jens Bergensten stopped seeing themselves as game programmers and instead focused on developing the game as a social platform.

That's a job description few game programmers would sign up for, and perhaps Pakman senses that his reasoning is approaching a sensitive subject, because he apologizes:

"It's hard to say that anything about *Minecraft* should be different, because it hasn't exactly hurt Mojang to do things as they have. For them, it's a question of identity. Markus describes himself as a game maker, not as a creator of social and creative platforms, and of course, he should continue to do so," he says.

Alex Leavitt finds just these kinds of discussions fascinating. Musicians, filmmakers, sculptors, architects, and game designers are all driven by the will to create, he says. To give shape to an idea and put their own stamp on it. Traditionally, the emphasis is on the individual creator—the artistic genius, the gifted musician, the visionary film director, or the game designer—as an elevated and respected person. To Leavitt, *Minecraft* questions that very view of artistic creation.

"How much of what *Minecraft* is today can be traced

to Notch and how much is the result of the interplay with the community? There's a tug-of-war there, between the creator's vision and the users' visions, which I think is very interesting."

Leavitt isn't the only one thinking along these lines. So is Jens, especially since he began working full-time on *Minecraft*. Jens is a typical programmer. What he likes best is to sit undisturbed, hunched over the keyboard, with plenty of time to develop the *Minecraft* world as he pleases. He is also a very creative person. He loves the artistic aspect of making games, programming new monsters maybe, or rewriting the code that determines how waterfalls work. When asked what he is most proud of in the game, he mentions the code he's written for generating underground caverns. In Version 1.2 of *Minecraft*, (released in winter 2012), Jens added house cats to the game. He got the idea from thinking about his own cat, Newton, at home in his apartment.

However, as *Minecraft* grows larger, Jens's job becomes more about making it easier for others to create and less about doing it himself. On Mojang's long "to-do list," two things are currently at the top: new functions for multiplayer games and an official plugin API, an interface that lets players program their own functions into *Minecraft* without permission from Mojang. These are functions

A replica of the Eiffel Tower in Paris, built on the popular FyreUK server.
By FyreUK (www.fyreuk.com) (www.youtube.com/user/fyreuk)

High Rossferry, a city of skyscrapers, bridges, and parks built entirely in *Minecraft*.
By Dydtor and Darkone (www.highrossferry.blogspot.com)
   (www.youtube.com/user/highrossferrycity)

The city is surrounded by water and connected to the mainland by bridges. The
architecture is inspired by US cities such as New York and Chicago.
By Dydtor and Darkone (www.highrossferry.blogspot.com)
(www.youtube.com/user/highrossferrycity)

A beachfront village with an ark, inspired by the biblical story of Noah. Built in survival mode on the Mindcrack server.

By BdoubleO (www.youtube.com/bdoubleo100) and Guude (www.youtube.com/guudeboulderfist) http://www.youtube.com/bdoubleo100

A wizard's castle and an eastern-style palace, with lava curtains activated on a day/
    night cycle. Built in survival mode on the Mindcrack server.
By Arkas (www.youtube.com/arkasmc) and W92baj (www.youtube.com/w92baj)

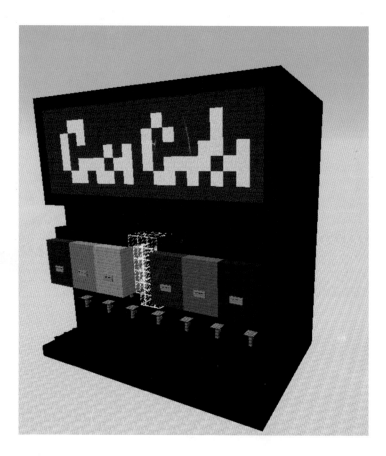

Fully functioning soda machine. Dispenses various cleverly named potions for the
    player.
By SethBling (www.youtube.com/user/sethbling) (twitter.com/SethBling)

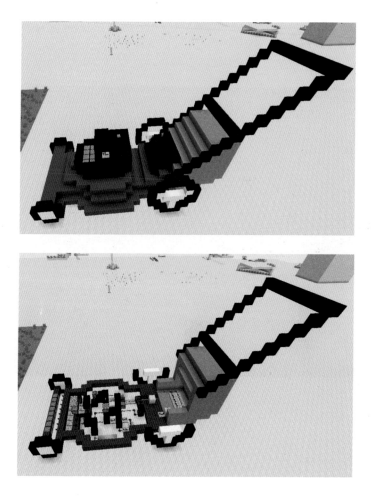

A working lawnmower, constructed using redstone.
By SethBling (www.youtube.com/user/sethbling) (twitter.com/SethBling)

A fleet of ships traveling through space, part of a series of space-themed maps.
By The VoxelBox (www.youtube.com/voxelboxvideos) (www.twitter.com/voxelbox)

A shrine built in the fantasy world of Nefret'Mizir, influenced architecturally by
  Persian styles and colors.
By The VoxelBox (www.youtube.com/voxelboxvideos) (www.twitter.com/voxelbox)

A temple built to resemble "Notch," the creator of *Minecraft*. Will dispatch various items to the player.
By Disco (www.youtube.com/fvdisco)

A fully playable *Minecraft*-remake of the classic '90s video game *Sonic the Hedgehog*.
By Disco (www.youtube.com/fvdisco)

A modern-style manor built in a small valley. The design is based around straight lines and cubic forms, with lots of open windows to maximize light.
By Aurelien Sama (www.youtube.com/user/AurelienSama) (twitter.com/ Aurelien_Sama)

An organic cathedral made out of mountains and trees.
By Aurelien Sama (www.youtube.com/user/AurelienSama) (twitter.com/Aurelien_Sama)

A volcano built on a tropical island, with several canyons and ravines.
By Aurelien Sama (www.youtube.com/user/AurelienSama) (twitter.com/
  Aurelien_Sama)

Herobrine's mansion, a popular adventure map with boss fights and customized monsters.
By Hypixel and Gazamo (www.hypixel.net)

Herobrine's Origins, an adventure map that uses redstone to present the player with
   challenges and puzzles.
By Hypixel and Mithrintia (www.hypixel.net)

that players have asked about for years, but they are far from the waterfalls, squids, and house cats that Jens otherwise so eagerly talks about.

We ask him what he would most like to do. If he could choose to work only with the pieces of *Minecraft* that he thinks are the most fun, what would they be? He ponders a bit before answering.

"It's more fun to create my own stuff. But I've realized that I can't compete with the whole world in coming up with the best features."

He's silent for a while, then adds, a little sadly, "We need to get started on things we've talked about but never got around to doing. Now that the game is officially finished, it suddenly feels a little urgent. We can't just fool around any longer."

Alex Leavitt laughs when he hears about Jens's thoughts.

"That's exactly spot on. These developments are new and very interesting. But for anyone working creatively, they are also a little depressing."

CHAPTER 12

TOO MANY FOR TWO PIZZAS

IN MARCH 2011, about six months after the dinner at Ljunggrens, Carl, Markus, and the others at Mojang took a couple of days off to go to the Game Developers Conference (GDC), in San Francisco. Every year, GDC attracts tens of thousands of people to a weekend devoted to panel discussions, game demonstrations, and networking. Amateur developers, who've saved up for months to fly there, mingle with the big bosses from Sony, Microsoft, and Electronic Arts; journalists; and legendary game developers.

Before the trip, they'd considered how they could market their game effectively at the conference. There are many interesting things to see at GDC. To get journalists to listen and business colleagues to notice you, you need to offer something extra. But what? The game's main character, Steve, had already become somewhat of a cult figure in indie circles, so someone had the idea to simply print Steve's face on cardboard boxes and make holes for the eyes, thus creating fun, characteristic *Minecraft*-like headgear. Besides being cheap to produce, the Steve masks could be flattened out and piled up, making them easy to transport to the United States.

To spice up the stunt, Markus and the others tweeted that only those who visited Mojang's little booth wearing blue T-shirts (the color Steve wears in *Minecraft*) would be able to take home a Steve mask. Carl ordered a hundred "Steveheads." It was a lot, he thought, but they could always find some use for the leftovers.

Now Carl stood bent over a boxful of cardboard heads, turned toward the wall in the little booth that Mojang had erected at GDC. Behind him, he heard the buzz from the convention floor, but was busy unpacking and assembling masks. The room was hot, he was sweating, and his back began to hurt. Also, he was worried that no one would show up. True, *Minecraft* had received a lot of attention in development circles, and Mojang was now making more money every week than most small developers made in a whole year. But at GDC, they were competing for attention with some of the giants of the business. This year game designer John Romero was revealing what had happened behind the scenes when the classic shooter *Doom* was created. Dustin Browder, the man responsible for some of the world's most popular strategy games, was talking about the philosophy behind *StarCraft 2*. At the same time, Nintendo's top man, Satoru Iwata, was showing the latest entry in the *Zelda* series, one of Nintendo's most important game series. Would anyone care about an odd little game from Sweden? Carl focused on the cardboard box in front of him. Regardless, the masks needed to be folded, and as CEO for a small startup company, he had to be prepared to step in where needed.

His anxiety didn't last long. When Carl stood up to stretch his back, he turned out toward the convention floor for the first time. In front of him was an ocean of people, all with their faces turned toward Mojang's booth, all wearing blue T-shirts. They looked like one swelling wave of people. Carl didn't get the chance to count, but it was pretty clear that there were considerably more than a hundred of them. Mojang's batch of Steve heads was gone in minutes.

During the winter of 2011, *Minecraft* went from being a well-liked indie game to becoming a sensation. Awards and honors rained on Mojang. Markus and his colleagues returned home from GDC with five shiny trophies in their luggage. Among other things, *Minecraft* was awarded for Best Innovation, Best Debut, and Audience Favorite. "I am so happy now you wouldn't believe it," Markus tweeted on the way home from the conference. On January 12, *Minecraft* surpassed one million copies sold. Hardly three months later, the number had doubled. Each day, Markus left work tens of thousands of dollars richer.

In the midst of all this, Markus, Jakob, and Carl stood with one single unfinished game on the merit list and a newly founded company to nurture. They had huge ambitions and lots of plans to put into action. Several new people had been hired, and the work on *Minecraft* continued. But most of all, the trio was just trying to keep a solid foothold in the circus that was spinning around them.

On one occasion, the Internet legend Sean Parker popped in at their headquarters on Södermalm. The man who had started the music site Napster a decade earlier and later became one of the top directors at Facebook and one of Silicon Valley's best-known investors listened with curiosity to Markus, Carl, and Jakob describe the company they ran together and their plans for the future. When asked if they would consider accepting a small investment, Carl answered politely but firmly no—Mojang didn't need money. Sean Parker shrugged his shoulders and thanked them, but before he left the office, he asked if the three guys had any plans for the evening. He'd been invited to a party and was looking for some company.

It was not an issue that the party in question was at the celebrity club The Box Soho, in central London. Naturally, Sean Parker had his private plane waiting at Stockholm Arlanda Airport. Markus, Carl, and Jakob tried their best to conceal their excitement as they hopped in a cab to the airport and the American millionaire's waiting jet. At three thirty the next morning, they stumbled out of the nightclub in London and got on the first available flight home to Stockholm. They got about an hour's sleep before it was time for the next meeting at the office.

"I feel like James Bond," wrote Markus on his blog the following day.

Over the summer, Markus and Elin found time to get married. The couple was traditionally attired at the wedding, but Markus kept his black fedora on. Mojang celebrated with a "wedding weekend," during which each person who bought *Minecraft* got a free copy "to give to someone you love."

The publicity surrounding *Minecraft* also meant that other companies began to contact them. Before GDC, cell phone manufacturer Sony Ericsson had asked them to find time for a meeting while at the conference. On-site in San Francisco, three representatives from Mojang found themselves in an air-conditioned conference room with four directors from Sony Ericsson, discussing a *Minecraft* version for the Swedish-Japanese company's cell phones. Seated around the table were Carl; Daniel Kaplan, Mojang's business developer; and programmer Aron Nieminen, recently hired to develop a *Minecraft* cell phone app.

Among the others at Mojang, Aron is known as "the smart one." In a company almost completely composed of programmers, it's a significant title. He and Markus got to know each other at Midasplayer, where they worked together on a couple of games. Even then, Markus had noticed Aron's head for math, which made him an unusually fast and effective programmer. When Mojang decided to develop a cell phone version of *Minecraft*, Markus sought out and recruited his old colleague for the task. Aron is also known for his knitted wool cap, which he wears indoors, outdoors, and at meetings with top directors of big corporations, such as the one he now found himself in.

The Sony Ericsson bosses laid their cards on the table. Later that year, the company would be releasing the Xperia PLAY cell phone, which is specially adapted for games. The Swedish-Japanese company was hard pressed by the competition, and that many Swedes continued to buy their cell phones was poor consolation when Sony Ericsson was losing its grip on the world market. The company heads had a good reason to curse out Apple in particular, whose iPhone had, in just a few years, become the phone everyone wanted. They needed a new start and a big hit, especially among younger buyers.

Mojang had something the directors of Sony Ericsson desperately needed: a cool game that everyone was talking about. What could be better to spark interest for their new gadget than a special version of *Minecraft*? If Mojang would consider developing the game, Sony Ericsson would gladly pay well for it, the directors told them. The only problem was time. Xperia PLAY would be premiered at the E3 Expo, barely three months away. Would it be possible to put together anything at all, even a playable demo, by then?

The other people in the room turned to Aron, who'd been sitting quietly in his cap, listening. He had only been working at Mojang for a couple of days. Before GDC, there hadn't been time for him to take even an initial look at the code that ran *Minecraft*. Now he would have less than ninety days to write a completely new version of the game, more or less from the ground up and for hardware that hadn't been released yet. Was it even worth a try? The young math genius leaned back in his chair and glanced up at the ceiling. Carl figured that he was calculating silently to himself. The directors of Sony Ericsson cast uneasy looks at one another. A couple of quiet seconds later, Aron looked down from the ceiling toward the others seated around the table.

"Okay, it'll work," he said.

Three months later, at the E3 Expo in Los Angeles, Carl looked on contentedly as Sony Ericsson exhibited *Minecraft* as the big news of the year, complete with a TV ad campaign in which the comedienne Kristen Schaal presented the game. "I made my face out of diamonds once and I passed out because it was so gorgeous," she said.

One of Carl's sharpest memories from E3 was when he stood at the top of an escalator and looked out over the showroom floor of the expo. Below him, a huge crowd milled around. He wondered at first where they were going, what new game was being shown that was drawing so many people. Then he caught a glimpse of a familiar black hat in the middle of the crowd. People had swarmed to Markus, who was trying to make his way across the show floor. The creator of *Minecraft* had become a superstar. E3 was the last time Markus moved about at a conference without a bodyguard at his side.

People who were in Markus's vicinity at this time describe him as happier than ever. But they also remember how the commotion stressed him out. With success always comes responsibilities, and with their big breakthrough, the Mojang guys were forced into making big, businesslike decisions for the first time. Often, they went against the playful, perhaps somewhat naive profile they most wanted associated with themselves and their company. At the E3 Expo, Mojang reached an agreement with Microsoft to develop a version of *Minecraft* for the Xbox 360. From a business perspective, the decision was a no-brainer. Around the world, there were close to 70 million Xbox 360 players. Microsoft also runs the online service Xbox Live Arcade, one of the most successful online game stores and the main source of income for thousands of indie game developers. Everyone involved expected *Minecraft* sales to get a huge shove toward the stratosphere when the Xbox version was released in May 2012. Carl would be able to add another couple of million to Mojang's already glowing revenue forecast.

On the other hand, it's difficult not to be reminded of the exact same world of corporate big business that Markus had done everything so far to avoid. The Xbox version of *Minecraft* was not developed by Mojang, but under license at the Scottish developer 4J Studios. The game was simplified and adapted to appeal to the broader, less geeky audience that Microsoft wants to reach. Specifically, the mystique around the crafting of tools and new minerals would be gone. The absence of documentation of exactly how different things are built in *Minecraft* was one of the most important reasons that such a large and living online community grew around the game. In the Xbox version, with the simple press of a key, the player can access a guide with all possible combinations laid out on the screen.

Markus also had to promise not to speak as openly

about the Xbox or Xperia versions of *Minecraft* as he'd done with his own earlier version of the game. His constant presence in the community had been a huge factor in the success of the game, but now he was to keep quiet about the details. The reason? Both Microsoft and Sony Ericsson paid for marketing the game and wanted control over what information would reach the public and how.

That particular promise is typical of the dilemmas that now plagued Mojang. Carl mentions accessibility and closeness to players as two of the company's greatest strengths. But now, interest in *Minecraft* was so enormous that its creator risked drowning in it. Every day, hundreds, perhaps thousands of questions, opinions, and suggestions inundate Markus. How do you maintain a close relationship with 20 million people?

A part of the solution is named Lydia Winters, online better known by her handle, Minecraftchick. In most contexts, she is completely unknown, whether she takes a walk in Stockholm or in her hometown of Saint Petersburg, Florida. But online, Minecraftchick is something of a phenomenon. Lydia belongs to the same group of Internet celebrities as The Yogscast and Captain Sparklez, but while others are praised for their impressive constructions or theatrics in the game, Lydia has made a name for herself thanks to her personality.

More than 60,000 people subscribe to her video blog on YouTube, where she posts a new video clip each week on a *Minecraft* theme. The most popular, where she explains the difference between various monsters in the world of *Minecraft*, has been viewed more than 800,000 times.

References to *Minecraft* run as a constant thread through Lydia's films and blog entries, but like many prominent bloggers, she has realized the value of letting her own personality permeate everything she does. The viewer who follows Lydia on YouTube learns more about her thoughts, views, and moods than he or she does about *Minecraft*. This is an extremely conscious choice. Her motto is to be personal and invite viewers into a dialogue. In her first films, she made a point of mentioning by name everyone who had written or commented on her earlier ones.

Lydia has always wanted to be a celebrity. As a child, she dreamed of becoming a singer or an actor. Growing up, she harbored ambitions of becoming a renowned photographer. Instead it was, more or less by chance, a peculiar game developed in Sweden that made her famous. In the autumn of 2010, Lydia's doctor informed her that she had an increased risk of developing breast cancer. She decided to start fund-raising for cancer research and started a campaign called "f/stop breast cancer," after the word for the aperture setting on a camera lens. The intention was for photographers to auction off mentorships and course time and donate the proceeds to research. To drum up interest, Lydia recorded her own video addressing the photographers she admired in which she talked about her plan and asked them to join the campaign. She also created a challenge: if she could raise at least $10,000, she would shave off her hair in front of the camera.

"F/stop breast cancer" became a talking point in the photography world. When it came time to tally the funds, Lydia found that she had raised more than $20,000. The YouTube clip where Lydia shaves off her hair has been viewed, as this book is being written, more than 90,000 times.

"I realized that things I did with video just worked," she says.

The breast cancer campaign taught Lydia the basics of how you attract attention on the Internet: be real, and find a gimmick. It also gave her an appetite for more of life as an Internet celebrity. If a film where she shaves off her hair could get so much attention, she thought, maybe she could turn it into a career? She decided to start her own YouTube channel. The only question was what the clips would be about. Lydia thought long and hard before some friends suggested *Minecraft*. It was a game she barely knew of, but that, according to what she had heard, was undoubtedly the next big thing on the web.

Two things made Lydia unique in the world she now entered: she is a woman, which is still relatively rare among gaming enthusiasts on YouTube; and she had never played *Minecraft* before. Her first films would be about how she took her first, shaky steps in the game. While others uploaded films of their most daring breakneck accomplishments and impressive buildings, she made entertainment out of her lack of experience. Her hair hadn't grown back out after the fund-raising campaign, and she'd bought a shocking-pink wig that she always put on before she turned on the camera. It swiftly became synonymous with the brand name Minecraftchick.

For Minecraftchick is just that: a brand name. Lydia didn't start playing *Minecraft* because she thought the game was fun. Rather, she understood the power and potential of connecting her name early on with a phenomenon that was exploding into popularity.

"I've always liked attention. Deep down, I believe, most people are like that. Having people read what I write and watch my films is a real kick," she says.

She had her first contact with Mojang just before the Swedes went to the E3 Expo. Lydia had contacted Carl, introduced herself, and asked if there was anything she could do to help. Most of all, she was trying to get a filmed interview with Markus. A chat with Notch would be a real scoop in the *Minecraft* world, and if she succeeded, her viewer ratings on YouTube would most likely skyrocket. The release with Sony Ericsson meant that Mojang needed all the help they could get, and Carl asked if she could stand in their shared booth. She would rave about how fantastically well *Minecraft* worked on the Swedish-Japanese cell phones.

When she arrived, Lydia noticed with disappointment that Markus didn't even seem to know who she was. He was surrounded by so many people that it felt hopeless to ask for an interview. But Carl saw her natural demeanor when speaking to people and offered her a job on the spot, on the condition that she would move to Stockholm.

"Only companies that don't have a community hire a community manager," said Carl, when asked about the job. So, Lydia was given the title Director of Fun. Even so, her job essentially entails taking care of the community that has grown around *Minecraft*. She was given the tasks of speaking with players on social media, organizing events, and being the company's public face.

No one who has seen Lydia speak in public can question her suitability for the job, but maybe her position at Mojang is also somewhat symptomatic. She was recruited because Markus, Jakob, Jens, and Carl don't have time to do what they themselves actually described as one of their most important jobs.

Jeff Bezos, the man who founded Amazon.com and one of the Internet business community's most influential people, has coined the expression "two-pizza team." That's a measure of how large a company that lives on creativity and new ideas should allow itself to become.

If a project group needs more than two pizzas to feed it, meaning between five and seven people, then it's too large, says Bezos. In a larger team, creativity and flow of ideas are limited and replaced with bickering and internal politics.

During the spring of 2012, Mojang hired its sixteenth employee.

As the millions rolled in and the number of *Minecraft* players grew that winter, these issues increasingly consumed Markus, Carl, and Jakob's time. How do you become a big company without becoming a big company?

There wasn't much in the numbers that was cause for worry, though. Mojang's revenue kept growing at an astonishing rate. From September 17, 2010, when the company was founded, to December 31, 2011, Mojang brought in a total of $78,722,300. Not too shabby, but for competitors and investors keeping an eye on Mojang, it was the company's profit margin that really impressed. Mojang's costs for the period were just over $8.7 million, including overhead. The remainder, more than $69 million, was pure profit. Markus's own company, Notch Development, directly received $60 million of it in license fees.

In the last few years, the whole Internet world has talked about the valuation of the new generation of Internet companies, defined as the sum an investor can reasonably be expected to pay for all the shares in a company. In other words, what the founders would get if they sold their company. The existing climate on the market has meant that Internet companies are often valued at ridiculous amounts of money, mainly based on projected future potential. Which means that even companies that are not particularly profitable can have a high value if investors agree that they are likely to earn big money in the near future. The most well known example is Facebook, which was valued at the dizzying sum of $104 billion when it went public on the NASDAQ. The euphoria was subdued, however, when the newly introduced stock plummeted during the first days of trading. Calamity howlers began to talk about a bubble bursting.

Since Mojang has never taken onboard any investors, it's difficult to put an exact value for the company. But looking at other prominent Internet companies gives a good estimate. Zynga was valued at close to $9 billion when it went public. That is twenty-five times more than the company's profits, which were just over $285 million at the time. According to investors, a valuation of between twenty and fifty times the profit margin would not be unfeasible with a company such as Mojang. Using that model to calculate its market value if sold, Mojang would have a price tag of between $1.5 and $4 billion.

Carl just shakes his head when numbers like these are mentioned. And perhaps there are more down-to-earth ways to measure how successful *Minecraft* has become than listening to the financial world's overly optimistic calculations. One way is to take a closer look at who is actually playing *Minecraft*, because the game is now used for much more than just entertainment. The best example of this is found on the other side of the Baltic Sea, deep in Finnish Karelia.

CHAPTER 13

MORE THAN A GAME

THE SMALL FINNISH town of Joensuu is located more than 200 miles northeast of Helsinki, barely an hour's drive from the Russian border. Most of the city's life revolves around the university there, one of Finland's largest, with more than fifteen thousand students. In the autumn of 2010, Santeri Koivisto was attending a teacher-training program there. He was almost twenty-five years old and had bigger plans for his career than becoming just another teacher in town.

One of his ideas was to combine two of his biggest

interests, computer games and education. In academic language, it's called game-based learning, a relatively new branch of education theory. Koivisto was fascinated by the thought of trying to harness the powerful attraction that computer games have on children and using it in the classroom.

The idea wasn't original. Many before Koivisto had tried to introduce games into schools to help increase students' interest. The concept of "edutainment," a cross between education and entertainment, was coined during the 1980s, when game developers realized that parents preferred to buy their children games that were educational as well as entertaining. In the nineties, boxes full of edutainment titles were sold, featuring popular animated characters that taught spelling, math, and history.

But Koivisto was far from impressed by what he'd seen so far. Messy math games and elementary vocabulary tests had nothing in common with the games that students played in their free time. It hardly felt worth the effort to investigate which of the existing games actually had an educational benefit. They were missing the most important thing of all—they were simply no fun.

In the winter of 2011, Koivisto read an article about *Minecraft* in the Finnish game magazine *Pelit*. He downloaded the game, installed it, and tried it out. Like so many others, he encountered a world where you could swiftly build pretty much anything. Just as typical, he couldn't put his finger on what the objective was.

But for an aspiring teacher in search of a game to take into the classroom, the lack of a goal and instructions was not disadvantageous. Koivisto saw *Minecraft*'s potential and decided to experiment with the game as a learning tool. He just had to find a class where the kids, parents, and school leadership would approve.

Just a little later, while winter still had Finland in an iron grip, he got a chance to put his ideas into practice. Outside of his studies, Koivisto sometimes worked as a substitute teacher in nearby Kontiolahti. One day, he stood in front of a class of ten-year-olds and asked if any of them had heard of *Minecraft*. Almost every hand flew up. Koivisto remembers in particular that almost as many girls as boys knew of *Minecraft*—something that could not be said of most computer games.

What *Minecraft* could contribute to the classroom experience was less than obvious. Finding something that the students are fond of isn't difficult, and neither is knowing what they need to learn. A teacher's challenge is to combine the two, and Koivisto was convinced that games in the classroom would be a way to succeed.

He explains his reasoning when we meet with him during a visit in Stockholm. In short, it's based on dissatisfaction with how most teachers run their classrooms today. "Most of them believe that students learn whatever the teacher writes on the whiteboard," he says.

Koivisto disagrees, and with that, he takes a stand in a pivotal question about how effective educational methods actually work. He speaks about the antiquated belief that children's brains absorb everything they are exposed to.

"Many teachers pile as much information as possible in front of their students and hope it goes in," he says. Koivisto recommends discussion and experimentation instead, letting students proceed by trial and error until they get results. Children can only learn when their brains are active, such as when they are actively discussing a subject or when they are totally attentive, like they are when trying to succeed in a game. Many would disagree, but it's clear that *Minecraft* fit very well into Koivisto's vision of how education should function.

In the classroom, Koivisto watched as the ten-year-olds clicked around, concentrating on the *Minecraft* world that he had built for them. There was still no version of the game designed for teaching, and each lesson had to be improvised using the standard version of the game. In the back of his mind, Koivisto began sketching larger plans.

Around the same time, Joel Levin was walking down West Ninety-Third Street in New York, on his way to work. He was a teacher at Columbia Grammar and Preparatory School in Manhattan, a private school near the city's most exclusive addresses on Central Park West. He taught computer skills to elementary school kids, and this spring, he wanted to try something new. After the winter break, he usually gave the students a new exercise using tools he found and liked on the Internet. The previous year, it had been Google Earth, and the lesson had been in geography. That wasn't his main area of expertise, but by letting the pupils learn about how to find countries with the help of the Internet, he made sure they would get their computer skills honed in the process.

Levin had been playing *Minecraft* for a few months, often at home in his apartment in uptown Manhattan, where he lived with his wife and two daughters, one and four years old. His first attempt at the game had gone so-so. He'd connected to an unmoderated game server and found himself in a world full of gigantic penis constructions and smashed castles. You couldn't even begin building before someone turned up and destroyed what you'd started or swiftly refashioned your creation into an impressive male organ of dirt and stone. It could have been worse, Levin reasoned. At least his kids hadn't been there to see it.

But he did have them with him later, when he'd found better servers to play on. His four-year-old daughter, Ellie, soon developed her own *Minecraft* habits. She navigated the game herself, but turned it over to dad for more complicated building, which he completed according to her instructions. The monsters were scary, so she asked him to turn them off in "the world game," as she called *Minecraft*.

One of his daughter's first solo projects in *Minecraft* was to build a tree house.

"You need to remember that we live in New York City. As long as she lives here, she will probably never build a real one," says Joel Levin.

The thought of using *Minecraft* in school had taken root in Joel's mind at the same time that Santeri Koivisto was making his plans in Finland. Levin's ambitions were initially humble. If nothing else, he thought, *Minecraft* could teach the students to use a mouse and keyboard. The blocky and relatively simple *Minecraft* world would be a suitable first step into a 3-D environment. If they wanted to build more complicated constructions, they would need to get out onto the web and learn more. During the first week, maybe he would give them the task of building their own stone pickaxes.

He brought the game to school on a chilly day early in the spring semester. His intention was to experiment with *Minecraft* for a couple of weeks, to see what it contributed to his classes and if the students learned anything. *Minecraft* remained a component of computer class for the rest of the year. The earliest lessons were no more complicated than giving the children the task of building something according to his instructions. Once they had learned to navigate and complete the simplest kind of building, the task was to go online and find information about how a certain material or tool could be made.

During another class, Levin built a golden pyramid that the kids could only get into if they helped solve a puzzle. Inside the golden pyramid were tiny, pixel-built ancient treasures. The first students to solve the puzzles and get to the treasures of course wanted to pick them up and escape with their loot. But Levin, noticeably proud, recounts the discussion that sprang up in the classroom. If you were to find antique objects in real life, he asked his students, would you just take them? Without having been there, it's impossible to say if it was really the kids' own idea, but Joel Levin says that, after some deliberation, his students finally arrived at the decision to build a museum, safeguarding the treasures instead of committing digital grave robbery.

Levin was worried that parents would think he was wasting their children's time playing unnecessary games in school. He was careful to limit *Minecraft* to being strictly a part of the curriculum, and even wrote a letter to the parents asking them not to buy their own copies of the game for home, at least not yet. *Minecraft* would be something that the kids did during class.

"In the beginning, I needed an excuse to use the game. It's not that way anymore."

Back to Karelia. Santeri Koivisto didn't really know where his experiment would lead, but the school principal had been positive about him trying out the new game in class. In contrast, to his colleagues at the university he was basically a laughing stock. Most of them thought it was a terrible idea, and even his adviser recommended he abandon the project. And yet, his students liked their new tool. The only thing left for Koivisto to do now was convince everyone else. After unveiling his plans at the annual Joensuu science fair, Sci-Fest, a discussion began online about introducing *Minecraft* into the schools. One of those who discovered what was happening in Finland was Joel Levin in New York. Another was Carl Manneh in Stockholm.

Most people who are sure they've had a stroke of genius are terribly disappointed when they find out that someone else has already discovered the same thing. That's exactly what happened to Santeri Koivisto when the teacher at the private school in Manhattan e-mailed him and enthusiastically described what he'd been doing in his own classroom. Once Koivisto's disappointment over not being unique had passed, the two of them proceeded to talk about the possibilities of collaboration.

They immediately agreed on a few points. *Minecraft* must be adapted to teachers' classroom needs in order to work well in schools. The world the students scampered around in had to be controllable, the monsters would have to be taken out, and they needed a way for teachers to supervise specific tasks, or else the project would never amount to more than unusually entertaining lessons for those kids who were already devoted gamers. The game needed to be rewritten and that wouldn't be possible without help from Mojang. This would turn out to be easier than they imagined. Once they got in touch, Carl Manneh immediately jumped onboard, asked them to start planning, and drafted up a reseller license agreement, the first and only one that exists for *Minecraft*. Carl's only condition was that the new version of *Minecraft* wouldn't just be about education, because then it wouldn't be fun.

The *Minecraft* code needed to be chopped up and reconfigured into a version where the teacher could control what happened in the game. Santeri Koivisto convinced Aleksi Postari, an IT student in his twenties, to spend his summer modifying the game. The custom mod he developed was given the academic-sounding name MinecraftEdu. The retail agreement with Mojang gave Koivisto a few euros for each copy sold and he began traveling around to schools, introducing MinecraftEdu to teachers and training those who wanted to try it for themselves. Santeri and Aleksi handled the transactions with their newly founded company, TeacherGaming, and brought on Joel Levin as a partner. At that point, the two Finnish students had never met the teacher from Manhattan in person. TeacherGaming board meetings were held via Skype or on a chat forum. None of them had met Carl either, or anyone else at Mojang.

Initially, Santeri Koivisto had no idea what his experiment with *Minecraft* in schools would lead to. Maybe he could add a couple of conclusions to his thesis or maybe just make a little money, he thought.

"Now I wake up in the morning and I've sold fifteen hundred dollars' worth of licenses. You realize that, yes, it might turn into something big," he says, and smiles a little awkwardly.

MinecraftEdu was an unusual success among educational games. In just the few first months after starting out, TeacherGaming sold Minecraft to enough schools to reach more than 100,000 students. At first it was just Finnish schools, but now there are teachers in Great Britain, the United States, Australia, and China using the game. By meeting with teachers in Minecraft, Santeri Koivisto and Joel Levin are able to hold courses where they demonstrate the possibilities that the game has to offer.

It isn't easy to explain why so many teachers have adopted *Minecraft*. The question of whether computer games contribute anything to instruction is even more difficult to answer. For the uninitiated, it sounds strange—playing games is something children do in their free time, isn't it? Hundreds of teachers the world over disagree, instead finding games a valuable learning tool for their students.

To find an explanation, we need to consider *Minecraft's* open-ended design, which lets teachers quickly build up the surroundings they need for particular lessons. Some of the first experiments in Finnish schools tried to show how deserts are created when trees are chopped down, a process that isn't very difficult to simulate in *Minecraft*. Other teachers have experimented with building models of molecules with *Minecraft* blocks. Obviously, the same thing can be achieved using other tools, but if kids feel more at home in *Minecraft* than with plastic models, why not meet them on home ground?

We find a similar example in the shabby, gray concrete giants of the Swedish government's housing projects in Stockholm's suburbs. Many of these properties, developed in the sixties and seventies, are now badly in need of renovation. Politicians argue over the best way to finance the task and about how the areas should look when finished. And there's at least as much squabbling about how the tenants in these areas will be able have their say in the design of their buildings, parks, and streets. Through an initiative of the company Svensk Byggtjänst, property owners in Fisksätra, Nacka, and Södertälje, south of Stockholm, have used *Minecraft* to help them solve these problems. The project was introduced under the name "My neighborhood." A *Minecraft* server was created, accessible to anyone. With the help of Mojang, Svensk Byggtjänst contacted experienced *Minecraft* builders, who began to construct a typical Swedish mass-produced suburb inside the game. Everything in it is made of the typical *Minecraft* blocks, which makes it easy to hack away pieces and put them somewhere else. Thus, one part of the neighborhood can get a makeover or one building can be torn down and replaced with another.

With the blocky suburb in place, Svensk Byggtjänst invited young people and put them in front of computers with a server connection. The participants were set free to build or tear down as they pleased, or to "visualize ideas," as the sponsors prefer to call it. Since then, several similar seminars have taken place. The construction company Telge-Hovsjö was one of the first to take heed of this odd way of city planning and other projects, and plan to be the first company in the world to use sketches and drawings done in *Minecraft* in their formal construction documents for a future project.

Joel Levin loves examples like these. He thinks of *Minecraft* as a Trojan horse. The game lets him sneak education into an environment where the students feel at home. Similar to the way *Minecraft* makes it more fun to plan cities, it helps Levin get students to show an interest in subjects they would ordinarily tire of after a couple of minutes. In academic language, this is called "gamification": the use of the motivation techniques and reward structures that are built into all good games to enliven tasks that would otherwise be insufferably boring.

Carl Manneh is quick to bring up both MinecraftEdu and the construction project in Fisksätra when he talks about *Minecraft*. He is clearly proud to be a part of what Santeri Koivisto and Joel Levin are doing. There are probably several reasons for this. Before he entered the Internet business, Carl worked as a substitute teacher, so he knows how difficult it can be to motivate bored students to care about what happens on the whiteboard in front of them. If MinecraftEdu is successful, it would be a huge step in making Mojang's enormous success about more than just entertainment. Creating the year's most talked-about and lucrative Internet company is one thing. Changing everyday life for students and teachers in classrooms around the world is something entirely different. Much more important, some would say. Maybe a small part of Carl agrees.

CHAPTER 14

BECOMING A LEGO

MARKUS WAS TIRED but happy when he returned home from the E3 Expo in Los Angeles. He'd been surrounded constantly, mingling with gamer fans and business VIPs alike. Still, it was nice to be back home. Everything was going exactly as he'd hoped at Mojang. Everyday life had settled in at the office. Normal mornings at the Mojang premises didn't completely live up to the playhouse picture suggested by its interior design. There was music on low in the background and the programmers were focused at their computers, the graphics people hunched over their screens.

That's not to say the workplace was always quiet. Discussions could become heated in the office and, thanks to the company's maximally liberal Twitter policy, reach far beyond the building. One major topic of debate during 2011 concerned a dragon. Most classically designed computer games have an endgame boss, the biggest, most difficult and final monster to be conquered before the game is completed. Markus felt that *Minecraft* needed something like that. Fans had been clamoring for an end boss for a long time, and in an interview Markus had said in passing that you should be able to "kill a dragon or something."

Jens lashed out, one of the few instances when the two didn't agree about how the game should develop. Dragons are (and this is a view he stolidly stands by to this day) a boring and unimaginative choice. But a dragon it would be. By *Minecraft* standards, the one they designed was an impressive creature—large, black, and with wings that, in spite of their blocky shapes, moved softly up and down when the creature flew.

Most of the employees were on vacation in the summer. The spring had been intense, and only a few months later it would be time for another trip to the United States, when the finished version of *Minecraft* would be released at MineCon in Las Vegas. A lot needed to be done before then.

Jakob had taken his family to Gotland to relax. At MineCon, he and the others would also show a playable version of *Scrolls* for the first time. The game had already received a ton of attention in the games press. A lot of people wanted to know what Mojang would do after *Minecraft*. Plenty of work on the new game remained; Jakob knew that many long days at the office awaited him when he returned from his vacation.

In another part of the world, there was already feverish activity concerning *Scrolls*. In the city of Rockville, Maryland, a group of lawyers hired by the game company ZeniMax had had turned their gaze toward Jakob's new game. ZeniMax is a large publisher, with many well-known game studios in its stable. Among them are id Software, which developed legendary games like *Doom* and *Quake*; and Bethesda Softworks, with the role-playing series *The Elder Scrolls* on their merit list.

The Elder Scrolls-series has occupied a special place in the hearts of many gamers since the first part was released in 1994. The games are gigantic, meticulously detailed adventures in a fantasy world, always created with player freedom as the guiding design principle. There are powerful dragons, armored knights, and flame-wielding magicians, loads of secrets to discover and treasures to plunder. In an *Elder Scrolls* game, players explore the world at their own pace and can choose the order in which to accept tasks and challenges.

The series is one of Markus's favorites, and it's fair to assume that *The Elder Scrolls* was among the inspirations when he and Rolf Jansson began designing *Wurm Online*. Now Bethesda was working on finishing the next *Elder Scrolls* game, titled *Skyrim*. Just like hundreds of thousands of others, Markus and Jakob had planned to spend a good part of the winter in front of their screens with the game.

But the fact that Mojang had landed in the sights of ZeniMax had little to do with *Skyrim*, and even less to do with *Minecraft*. The corporate lawyers had noted the similarity between the name Mojang had chosen for its next project and their series. Too similar, they felt, and decided to do something about it.

Jakob had just returned from vacation when a letter from ZeniMax arrived at the office. It contained a document fifteen pages long and written in complicated legalese. But the central message was unmistakable. According to ZeniMax's lawyers, Mojang was not allowed to name its game "*Scrolls*." It was so similar to the name of Bethesda's series that they regarded it as a trademark infringement. Change the name, the American company advised them starkly. If they didn't, the case would go to court.

This wasn't the first time the American company had been in contact. Earlier in the fall, Mojang had applied for a trademark for the title *Scrolls*. It had been mostly to test the waters. Neither Jakob nor anyone else at Mojang had any idea whether you could really trademark a single word. It didn't take long before ZeniMax contacted them asking about the project. Even then, the Americans made it clear that they considered the title a problem. From ZeniMax's point of view, the two names—*Scrolls* and *The Elder Scrolls*—were too similar.

Markus and Jakob wanted to avoid a conflict. They immediately suggested a subtitle for their own game. They would even consider skipping the trademark (but still call their game *Scrolls*), if it would get ZeniMax off their backs. The American lawyers rebuffed both suggestions, but didn't send an immediate counteroffer. Everything went quiet after that. Jakob figured the issue was settled. The letter from ZeniMax he now held in his hand proved otherwise, beyond the shadow of a doubt.

The board of Mojang—Markus, Carl, and Jakob—met to discuss what they should do about it. They decided that the best defense is a good offense. Just folding and "letting them kick us around," as Jakob puts it, was never an option. Mojang's next game would be named *Scrolls*, no matter the cost.

Initially, it was difficult for them to take the lawsuit seriously. In a blog posting, just a few weeks after the threat of a lawsuit dropped through the mail chute, Markus suggested another way of resolving the conflict.

"I challenge Bethesda to a game of *Quake 3*. Three of our best warriors against three of your best warriors. We select one level, you select the other," he wrote in a blog post. "If we win, you drop the lawsuit. If you win, we will change the name of *Scrolls* to something you're fine with."

He never received an answer. Another time, Carl tried to resolve the whole deal with an e-mail to Robert Altman, the top boss at ZeniMax. Can't we just meet and try to work this out, he suggested, offering him a cup of coffee.

"I'm not interested in coffee," was the short reply.

In September, ZeniMax submitted its formal complaint to Stockholm's district court. Many of the developers who worked for Bethesda were ashamed of their mother company's actions, especially since they—like most others in the business—were full of admiration for what Mojang had done with *Minecraft*.

"This is a business matter based on how trademark law works, and it will continue to be dealt with by lawyers who understand it, not by me or our developers," said Bethesda's marketing director, Pete Hines, in an interview. Markus expressed himself in similar terms.

"I am a huge fan of Bethesda's work, and I am looking forward to *Skyrim* more than I am any other game this year," he wrote in an e-mail to the gaming site Kotaku.com.

It was Carl's job as CEO to solve the problem, but it had the greatest impact on Jakob. When he and Markus had started Mojang the year before, the two projects came side by side: *Scrolls* from Jakob and *Minecraft* from Markus. Markus's game concept was already one of gaming history's biggest hits, but Jakob's contribution hadn't even left the drawing board yet. Jakob had begun to feel anxious. How would Mojang's millions of fans—who loved *Minecraft* more than any other game—receive his project? Eventually, the commotion around Markus's game would subside. Then it would be important to have something new to show.

It was not likely that *Scrolls* would be as big a success as *Minecraft*. Everyone involved was careful to stress that. But it was important to show the world that Mojang was more than a one-hit wonder. Jakob was convinced that *Scrolls* would do the job. If it flopped, he would have to take the blame.

For Jakob, the legal process with ZeniMax came to represent everything he hated about the established game industry. As a child, he'd dreamed of becoming a lawyer, but his dealings with the Zenimax legal team felt nothing like like the heroic agents of justice he remembered from his childhood evenings in front of the TV.

Trademark disputes are a dime a dozen in the business world. This case would probably have passed unnoted if it hadn't involved two such different parties. In one corner stood Mojang, the most highly praised indie developer in the gaming world. In the other, the huge company,

Jakob Porser. Photo by Elin Zetterstrand.

ZeniMax, with several enormously popular games in their portfolio and an army of attorneys at their disposal. You might see the battle between Mojang and ZeniMax as pure harassment, a giant company using legal brawn to protect its revenue and repress a startup. That was exactly how the employees at Mojang felt, and it was the story that created headlines in the gaming press during the summer.

Or you could see it as Mojang's first real encounter with the world of big business, which they inescapably were becoming part of. Regardless of Markus's self-image, ZeniMax had long since ceased to view Mojang as a harmless little indie company. Mojang was pulling in several million dollars and was one of the gaming world's most talked-about companies. For ZeniMax, the creators of *Minecraft* weren't innocent startups. They were perfectly valid competitors.

In October, just weeks before MineCon in Las Vegas, Mojang won an important first victory. The Stockholm District Court threw out ZeniMax's demand for a so-called temporary injunction, which would have prevented Mojang from using the name "*Scrolls*" during the term of the court case. In the ruling, the court states that the names are not easily confused. ZeniMax could have withdrawn its charges then, but the publishing company stuck to its guns. Now what remained was either a trial or a settlement.

As the court case dragged on, the attention surrounding *Minecraft* brought other things forward that Markus would have rather not thought about. In the autumn, *Aftonbladet,* a Swedish daily tabloid, published an interview with Rolf Jansson, Markus's old friend from his *Wurm Online* days. They only saw each other sporadically nowadays. His friendship with Rolf was just one of many things that Markus had been forced to put on the back burner in order to make time for everything concerning *Minecraft.*

Rolf still lived in Motala and now worked full-time with *Wurm Online.* Compared to most indie developers, he was doing quite well. The number of paying *Wurm Online* players was growing slowly but surely and had recently passed three thousand. Rolf made enough money to work full-time with the game and had even hired two more people at his firm. But he did miss working with Markus, and the success of *Wurm Online* did pale in comparison to that of *Minecraft.* About this time, Markus's game was attracting more new players daily than Rolf Jansson had scraped together in almost eight years. But *Wurm Online* was the game Rolf had always dreamed of creating; working on your dream is something only a few game developers can actually achieve.

The article in *Aftonbladet* painted a picture of Markus screwing over Rolf: Markus had stolen the best ideas from *Wurm Online* and taken them to his own game. Rolf never says it outright, but readers still get the impression that Markus's earlier collaborator was swindled out of both money and success. Markus comes across as being indifferent; he briefly answers only two of the reporter's questions and then explains his desertion as frustration over not being able to influence *Wurm Online* in the way he wanted.

The article stirred up strong emotions in both Markus and Rolf. They discussed it in a telephone conversation that ended on a bad note. Looking back both say that *Aftonbladet*'s article presented an inaccurate image of reality, but neither can really say in what way. Markus is satisfied with stating that things were "taken out of context." Rolf is very reluctant to answer questions about the whole thing, but offers this comment over the phone: "I am really glad that Markus has gotten rich. That comes from the heart. On the other hand, I'm not completely at peace with how it happened. I can't think of anything else to say."

Today, their friendship is complicated. Before, they could talk computer games for hours. Now they talk a couple of times per year, mostly on the phone, most often about business. Markus is still a partner in the company that runs *Wurm Online*. He is on the company board, but is careful to emphasize that he has no creative influence over the game. Their friendship has been replaced by a more "professional" relationship, as Rolf describes it.

It's obvious that as Markus's success has grown, the two have drifted farther away from each other.

Mojang was founded on a pronounced indie mentality. The company would be small and agile and would only spend time on projects in which the employees were interested. That attitude was central to the vision that Carl and the others expressed together. It was sort of a mission statement, formulated shortly after the dinner at Ljunggrens when the company was founded: Mojang was to become the world's most influential indie developer.

As the CEO of a successful, quickly growing company, it's surprising that Carl would be supportive of such an ambition. Their central vision said nothing about revenue, growth, high profit margins, or new markets— nothing about success in business. It's entirely possible to be influential without ever becoming rich (just ask Franz Kafka), and it must be said that Mojang rejects the easy money. A comparison with perhaps the most well-known cell-phone game in history, *Angry Birds*, illustrates that quite clearly. It was very deliberately developed into a giant industry with a steady stream of sequels, stuffed dolls, and a planned stock market introduction. Rovio, the company behind the game, exploited its new-won victory when sales shot up, and redefined itself from a small company with a handful of employees to a well-oiled machine, driven with laser precision by business-development principles. Nothing says that Mojang couldn't go in the same direction.

Jakob snorts when Rovio is mentioned, calling it a one-trick pony.

"They only have one game idea and that's actually a copy of an existing game, where they've inserted graphics from an old project. They had one hit, and now they're milking it like crazy."

There are two main reasons why Mojang's view of growth is different. First of all, the company was started around an existing success. The three owners decided which direction the company would take and used their own capital to take it there. Second, you need to take a look at who started Mojang. Jakob and Markus have never made a secret of their complete lack of interest in money matters. They are almost proud of not comprehending money, contracts, and things they associate with men in suits and ties. Carl seldom wears clothes different from what the others wear, but at the end of the day, it is still his job to be that man in the suit and tie. Markus has described the CEO's job this way: to take care of "the boring stuff," because Markus wants to stay busy with the fun stuff.

That's why there is no planned sequel to *Minecraft* or new levels available for download at an extra cost. According to the extant logic of the game business, the plans for *Minecraft 2* would have already been under way and there would be many expansion kits to get existing customers to pay once more. Instead, completely separate games, such as *Scrolls*, are growing within the walls of the company.

Investors who have been involved in some of Sweden's and the world's fastest-growing technology companies are completely baffled by this strategy. But they will only comment anonymously, probably because they are holding onto hopes of realizing future profits on Mojang's success.

"The cost of every missed opportunity to work with *Minecraft* is enormous," says one of them. "Every second they invest in something else takes time away from what they could be doing with *Minecraft*."

Carl's method for keeping his balance is to innovate around *Minecraft*, that is to say, alongside it, instead of squeezing the game into conventional business logic. Mostly, he hopes for a service that makes it simpler to play *Minecraft* with others online. Starting a server where several *Minecraft* players can meet and build together is notoriously complicated. Inventive businesses have for years offered professionally hosted servers for a fee. Now Mojang wants to do the same. Renting out official *Minecraft* servers would make playing the game easier, but it would also cure Mojang's big business weakness: customers who pay once and then expect free updates forever. If enough people were to go for it, it would give Mojang a steady source of income without the game's sanctity being compromised. The sights are set on 50 million players.

It is not easy for Carl to take Mojang in a different direction, and not just because Markus and Jakob own the lion's share of the company. It was free experimentation that led to the creation of *Minecraft*. Mojang was founded on the view of the game developer as an artist, with all the freedom and quirkiness that entails. That is what made it possible for everyone in that office on Åsögatan to live well on their success, not on business plans or market analyses or a carefully planned PR strategy. Carl knows all this. Perhaps his most difficult task is the balancing act of being CEO for a company that doesn't really want to be a company. At least, not in the same way as other companies are.

By the end of 2011, Mojang's influence on the gaming world was undeniable. The Internet was flooded with more or less obvious attempts to copy *Minecraft*'s success. Every word from Markus or one of the others at Mojang was elevated in the press to the status of prophecy. When Epic Games, well known for lavish war games such as *Gears of War* and *Unreal Tournament*, premiered its new title, *Fortnite*, the director of design, Lee Perry, mentioned *Minecraft* as one of their most important sources of inspiration.

But indie? Can you even be indie with over $70 million in the bank?

In winter 2012, Mojang struck a license agreement with Danish LEGO. Shortly thereafter, the first LEGO kits on a *Minecraft* theme popped up in stores. Markus's desk at Mojang was soon full of gray, green, and brown *Minecraft* LEGO bricks and small plastic LEGO Creepers. Markus, Jakob, Carl, Jens, and the others took part in the marketing campaign, even participating in a small ad that was uploaded onto YouTube.

It's not hard to imagine how moved Markus was when he held the LEGO pieces in his hand for the first time. No matter whom you ask, LEGO is always among the first things mentioned when the subject of Markus's childhood comes up. Furthermore, it's perhaps the clearest source of inspiration behind the game that made him a multimillionaire. But you can also turn that line of reasoning around and consider the LEGO toys as a sign that Mojang was moving in a different direction than its founders had intended. When asked what the most important thing is for his company, Markus always answers that it's to be able to do "exactly the games we want to." The goal is definitely not to become a Rovio (a cynical profit machine, in his eyes) instead of a company based on the love of good games.

To any outsider observing Mojang at this time, the difference was not so apparent. Like Rovio, Mojang made almost all its money on a single game, and like *Angry Birds*, *Minecraft* hasn't changed radically since its birth. Mojang's proceeds from merchandizing have soared. Via online shops, Mojang was selling T-shirts, posters, toy Creepers, foam-rubber pickaxes, refrigerator magnets— even baby onesies with *Minecraft* prints. In addition, there is talk of plans for Hollywood movies and contracts with several more toymakers. The more money that flowed in, the more obvious it was that *Minecraft* was changing. The game was on its way to becoming something that Markus could no longer control.

CHAPTER 15

"YOU DID IT, MARKUS. YOU REALLY DID IT."

WE ARE APPROACHING the end of the first day of MineCon in Las Vegas. The stage is still littered with the confetti Markus unleashed when he pulled the lever a couple of hours earlier, symbolically releasing the finished version of *Minecraft* to the public. The five thousand seats in the hall are empty. Now the audience is milling in the room next door, a space just as large but lacking seats. In one corner, the hotel personnel have installed a bar for serving drinks. The bartender picks around among the bottles, looking bored. Most of

Costume contest at MineCon 2011. Photo courtesy of Mojang.

the participants are much too young to drink alcohol. Besides, they're already flocking to the stage in one corner of the room for the cosplay contest, the highlight of the weekend for many, where fans dressed as *Minecraft* players compete for prizes.

"Let the squid through!" Lydia Winters shouts into the microphone, and a square person with knee-length arms stumbles forward through the audience. The finalists line up onstage, all dressed as figures from the game. Besides the squid, there is a human TNT-box, a female wolf in a bikini-like outfit, a huge green monster, and a skeleton dressed in a skintight leather suit. The front rows are filled with a hundred costumed fans who'd hoped to be invited up onstage. Most of them are dressed as Steve, *Minecraft*'s main character, each with a stone pick in hand.

Lydia Winters explains the rules to the boisterous audience. Voting will be done by shouting and applause from the crowd, and the contestant they shout the loudest for will be the winner. Lydia is the sole judge. With the patient voice of a kindergarten teacher, she repeats time and again that audience members may only shout and applaud once. She has her hands full with this rowdy bunch, both on and off the stage. On one occasion, the pressure is so great she is forced to ask everyone to take one step back. The scantily dressed wolf, already known as Wolfgirl, wins. If that has something to do with the high percentage of teenage boys in the room, we'll leave it unsaid. Wolfgirl is beside herself with joy; first prize is a lunch with Markus.

On the other side of the expo floor, between the huge red-eyed black dragon and the photo corner, where fans line up to pose with a six-foot-tall Creeper statue, a group of indie programmers is squeezed in. They are specially invited guests, T-shirt–wearing guys and girls in sneakers and jeans. They have all created games that Markus or someone else at Mojang likes and have been invited to MineCon to show what they're working on. Throughout the whole conference, they've been standing there, fidgeting while the audience pours into the room.

Some of their games are finished; others are not much more than sketchy demonstrations designed around a central idea. One booth displays *Closure*, a black and white puzzle game built by American programmer Tyler Glaiel. In *Closure*, players manipulate light and dark in order to travel through a dreamlike, sketchily drawn shadow world. Another booth offers a hard-to-fathom red-and-blue 3-D world on two side-by-side screens. This is a demo of British developer Terry Cavanagh's new title, *At a Distance*. The game is completely incomprehensible to a single player, but if two players collaborate and compare what they see on their respective screens, together they can figure out the purpose of the game.

Many who wander by cast curious glances at the creations shown. Some plod onward, most toward the shop to buy *Minecraft*-themed T-shirts, stickers, and paper helmets. Others stop and pick up a controller to try one of the games. They are met with proud smiles from the creators themselves, who guide players through their creations and demonstrate features of which they're extra proud.

In one corner, we meet James Green and Ken Klopp. They've come to MineCon from Seattle to exhibit their game, *AirMech*, the first produced by their company, Carbon Games. The two look like typical computer nerds—James is tall and skinny, with long, straight hair falling over his shoulders, while Ken is round and wears oversized glasses. And in many ways, *AirMech* is the ultimate nerd fantasy.

It's a postapocalyptic, three-dimensional strategy game, viewed from a bird's-eye perspective. The player controls an army of tanks and fighter planes that, with the push of a button, can transform into flame-and-bullet-throwing giant robots. The world of *AirMech* is embellished with hand-drawn manga-like graphics and filled with knowing winks to old game classics. The basic setup is borrowed from the cult classic *Herzog Zwei*, released for Sega Mega Drive in 1989. Among the units the player controls in *AirMech* is the *Minecraft* Creeper, a tribute to the hosts of MineCon.

Unlike many other indie developers, James and

Ken have a long background in the established game industry. They worked from the mid-1990s for the big-name Ubisoft on large-scale productions such as *Unreal Tournament*, *Splinter Cell*, *Far Cry*, and *King Kong* (based on Peter Jackson's blockbuster of the same name). In 2008, they moved to Epic Games China. There they developed *Fat Princess* on commission from Sony Computer Entertainment. It was released as a download for PlayStation 3 and unanimously praised by critics.

In spite of their successes, it was a strain to work for a large publisher. The pair was shot down when they proposed developing new features for *Fat Princess* and releasing it on more platforms. Since Sony owned the copyright and the developers didn't, James and Ken had little say about the decision. Their ideas for future projects were given the cold shoulder. Their ideas weren't in line with the company's strategy, they were told. Instead, James and Ken were asked to work on a game engine to run online games for the Chinese market.

That was nowhere close to what the two of them had dreamed of doing. In the summer of 2011, they took their savings and started Carbon Games. There, they would make the games they wanted to and release them for sale on their own, without having to navigate the bureaucracy of a large company.

"It's amazing. We can talk about the game whenever

we want and interact with the players. We decide how *AirMech* will work, what to develop, and when to release it," says Ken.

Now they're here in Las Vegas, exhibiting their creation for more than five thousand gamers, all thanks to the Swedish man in the hat whose own game became a worldwide sensation. The significance of *Minecraft* to the indie scene cannot be overstated, James and Ken say in chorus.

"For everyone else on the indie scene, *Minecraft* is a benchmark. It is a signal that shows that it is possible to breakthrough on their own. It does not take a lot of marketing or a large publishing company. Just a really good game that people are talking about," says James.

Of course, James and Ken are hoping that some of the thousands of people who paid to visit MineCon will also pay to play *AirMech*. It's mainly due to *Minecraft* that indie developers today even dare to think they might earn decent returns on their games. All the millions of players who bought *Minecraft* through Markus's homemade website have overcome a mental barrier, is what James Green and Ken Klopp figure. For those millions, buying a game no longer means visiting a store, taking down a cardboard box from a shelf, and paying a cashier. The transaction could just as likely happen on the Internet, buying a game from a completely unknown game developer, after getting a tip on Twitter, Facebook, or YouTube.

"I see *Minecraft* as a sign of the indie scene's big break-through. There has probably never been a better time than now to be game developers," says James.

Markus is sitting nearby in the same room and his hand is tired. He has written autographs for three hours already, and the line is still several hundred feet long, snaking through the room. Everyone wants Markus's signature on a T-shirt, backpack, or plastic pickaxe. Before he's had time to meet them all, his energy is depleted. Disappointed fans watch as he's led away through the masses by his bodyguard, a middle-aged man with gray hair, white shirt, and a stern countenance—a police officer before he took this job, we're told.

Maybe such security is needed. When Markus heads for the men's room, the bodyguard has to push and shove to keep the fans away. The door closes behind Markus so he can do his business in peace, but the mob of fans gathers outside. Soon there are hundreds, most of them brandishing cell-phone cameras in hopes of getting a glimpse of their idol when he emerges. A single expo visitor happens to be inside. He greets Markus politely. Markus hesitates before exiting.

Just over a year ago, Markus had printed and framed the account balance showing his first million kronor in the bank. Then it had felt like proof he hadn't gone mad, that all his hours in front of the screen had been worth it. Against all odds, his remarkable little game had found an audience.

Now, among the hordes of fans at MineCon, he's had time to acclimate to his wealth: now a million kronor is the equivalent of one day's average sales, over $150,000. If he so desired, Markus could spend the rest of his life on a sandy beach drinking cocktails.

In Sweden, that is very rare. But in Silicon Valley, a whole industry has arisen to cater to nouveau-riche entrepreneurs, offering not only to swab the decks of luxury yachts and deliver French vintage wines, but such services as psychological guidance for the suddenly wealthy.

Often, their clients are people who've worked at quickly expanding IT companies, with the usual stock options. When the company is sold or goes public, they are transformed overnight from programmers with normal salaries into multimillionaires. Suddenly, they no longer have any reason to go to work. Some of them buy new houses, some get new cars, and some become conflicted about their sudden wealth. At least, that is what San Francisco psychologists Stephen Goldbart and Joan DiFuria claim. They have coined the expression "Sudden Wealth Syndrome." Armed with the toolbox of psychology, they've spent their professional lives guiding people who are suffering from the syndrome. They even founded the Money, Meaning & Choices Institute, a company specializing in psychological guidance for this at-risk group.

There are most likely more crass reasons than altruism for psychologists to want to specialize in therapy for absurdly rich people. Newspaper articles about court cases brought about by sudden wealth were most common around the turn of the millennium, when the value of IT companies was most inflated. When the bubble burst, many psychologists quickly adapted. Those who'd previously offered treatment for Sudden Wealth Syndrome began to focus on its opposite, Sudden Loss of Wealth Syndrome.

It's easy to write off these psychologists as gold-digging opportunists. But that doesn't mean it wouldn't be overwhelming to go from wage earner to multimillionaire in a very short time. Joan DiFuria describes three aspects of the wealth problems in an interview: denial, shock, and finally, and perhaps the most interesting, the feeling of not being worth so much money.

Markus mentions it immediately when the subject of wealth comes up. Throughout his childhood and youth, he saw for himself what it means to have little money. The fights that ensued when he or Anna had caused the family sky-high telephone bills (Markus, because of his constantly used modem, Anna because she talked to friends) are among his strongest memories from childhood. On the other hand, he doesn't recall thinking of his family as particularly poor. In Salem, there weren't many rich families to be compared to. But it's clear that the contrast he now experiences has gotten him thinking. He wrings his hands when he talks about how he feels about his money.

"My job doesn't actually produce anything for society. I don't contribute food or anything like that. But I still make a lot more money than those who are truly needed. It is all because I can sell my product on the entire Internet. You can't do that when you bake bread."

Markus is very much aware that whether he gets out of bed or not, one day of *Minecraft*'s revenue is equal to what a nurse—like his mother—earns in four years. And yes, it bothers him some.

"I'm not complaining. It just feels a little backwards. I don't think that there is an evil conspiracy to keep wages down, but people are doing things that really mean something, and they still don't make any money."

The concept of financial independence has no strict definition. For some, it means having enough money in the bank to be able to live without using up one's savings, living on passive income in the form of interest and dividends from investments. Others see it as being rich enough to be able to have a reasonable standard of living for the rest of one's life. But regardless of how you twist and turn the words, *Minecraft* made Markus financially independent about a year and a half after it was first released. In the autumn of 2010, he'd earned around $7 million. That was before Mojang had acquired an office, a CEO, partners, and employees, so all that money went straight into Markus's own pocket. By late 2011, his personal fortune had increased tenfold.

There are plenty of stories about sudden riches that end in misery. Especially those about lottery winners who go from being broke to obscenely wealthy in literally one second, like the American mother of three who won $1.3 million a few years ago.

Before she won, she lived in a tiny apartment and worked four jobs in order to feed her family. When the money landed in her account, she bought a house and some new clothes, but she saved most of it. Then everything went wrong. A couple of years later, she told how letters begging for money, demands from relatives, and an obscene number of marriage proposals had completely overwhelmed her. She was threatened and accused by people who had previously been close to her. When CNN interviewed her, she asked the TV channel not to divulge her real name. She had had enough of the side effects of wealth.

"Sometimes I wish I could change my name and go somewhere and hide."

Those who savor Schadenfreude can find plenty of

material in tales like these; they usually end with the winners or someone close to them dying. But they don't change a basic fact of wealth—the research does confirm that we humans become happier when we have a large sum of money in the bank.

For Markus, the money was not rolling in as fast as it does for a lottery winner, but things happened quickly when the media got a whiff of the mysterious Notch and his millions. From being just a popular indie developer, in just a few months' time he became one of Sweden's most discussed individuals. Patiently, he answered the journalists' questions. No, he hadn't been blinded by the money. No, he hadn't spent it all on craziness.

When we speak with people close to Markus, they all maintain that the riches haven't changed him. Some say that it's because of his choice of friends; he has few instead of many, and most of them are slightly obsessive game developers rather than expensive-cocktail-drinking jet-setters. Others point out that Markus's success came gradually, over the period of a few years. A third explanation is that Markus's family has always kept him grounded. It would be a lie, however, to say that he's never been tempted by conspicuous consumption.

For instance, there was the time he sat at his computer, randomly surfing the web while taking a break from programming. On a shopping site he had stumbled upon, he saw a watch he liked. It had a classic design, really sharp.

And best of all, he could afford it. He called Elin, who looked over his shoulder at the screen.

Elin was silent for a while, looking at the price tag: $114,000.00.

"Markus, it's a watch. A watch."

After a short discussion, the purchase was averted. Markus realized that a gadget he would never dare wear was worthless anyway.

Many articles written about Markus's sudden wealth are about how it doesn't seem to have changed his behavior. He showed up for interviews in the same hat and clothes as before. One article mentions that he seemed to have been shopping on the way to the interview; the reporter noted that his bag was from Dressmann, a popular low-price chain in Sweden. But to a certain extent, Markus's spartan lifestyle is a myth. He and Elin have moved into an exclusive residence in central Stockholm.

In the spring of 2011, Markus began talking about taking his family on a trip. He needed a break from working on *Minecraft*. His sister, Anna, had been talking about taking her youngest daughter on a flight for the first time, maybe to Turkey, a destination that was within her budget thanks to the charter flights to the coast. Instead, Markus booked a private jet to Paris. When the plane took off, Markus's mother, Ritva, and Anna, accompanied by kids and fiancé, were aboard, along with Elin and her mother.

After a few days of sightseeing and shopping, they flew home. When the plane was in the air, Markus leaned over to his sister, as far as the seatbelt would allow.

"Is this fun?" he asked.

The question might seem strange, but Anna saw that her answer was important to Markus. The money that had dropped into his lap would, first and foremost, make it possible for him and his family to have fun. He needed an answer.

"Yes, this is fun," said Anna.

Five years had passed since Markus's sister had kicked her drug habit. Her path had been via therapy, a new partner, and children. She continued to go to AA meetings. Her job as a care assistant didn't pay very well, but she could live on what she earned. Now she was sitting back, gazing through the window of a private jet, on the way home from a trip to Paris.

Anna and Markus have an agreement when it comes to how he shares his wealth. She has promised never to beg for money from her brother. Of course, she'll gladly accept gifts, but it must always be Markus's initiative. Part of it is that she's afraid she'll become greedy and the money will destroy their relationship. Besides, she got herself clean and off the streets all by herself, not with the help of a rich relative. When she began to get her life together, the condition of her teeth remained visible evidence of her troubled past. But instead of strewing money over his sister, Markus paid her dental bills.

In less private contexts, Markus's fortune is a hot topic of speculation. Everyone who knows his background knows how important gaming is to him, and to developers, the thought that his money might finance other independent game is titillating. As a patron, Markus's millions would go far in bankrolling promising-but-broke developers. Besides, the money would be funneled back into the world Markus was a part of and perhaps form the foundation of future success stories. That's why many were overjoyed when he sent out a signal in early 2012 suggesting he was going to do just that.

It all began when famous game developer Tim Schafer wrote a few lines about wanting to do a follow-up to his game *Psychonauts*. *Psychonauts* had been released in 2005 and had been widely acclaimed by reviewers. Schafer, who in the nineties had worked at LucasArts on classic adventure games such as *The Secret of Monkey Island*, *Day of the Tentacle*, *Grim Fandango*, and *Full Throttle*, was already a legend in the gaming world. He was praised for his singular sense of humor and his ingenious way of telling stories with his games.

Even today, many people maintain that *Psychonauts* is one of the best games ever made. Markus is one of them. But *Psychonauts* was a commercial flop. Majesco, the publisher, lost a lot of money on it, and its CEO was forced to resign shortly thereafter. Among players who know their history, *Psychonauts* is a popular example of the moneyed publishers' total disinterest in games with artistic ambitions. Indie developers in a bad mood like to point to it as proof of the unfairness of the world.

Now, Schafer says, he would like to make a sequel. To do that, he would need "a few million dollars." With the memory of its predecessor's miserable sales still fresh, he understood that the chance of anyone financing his project was minimal. Until Markus piped up and openly tweeted, "Let's make *Psychonauts 2* happen." Everyone knew he could afford it, and what would be more beautiful than to use *Minecraft's* millions to give new life to a classic game? The gaming world was in a whirlwind over the story. We meet with Markus a few days later. He's already explained that the financing of *Psychonauts 2* won't happen. It turned out to be significantly more expensive than he'd expected, more money than the sequel could reasonably earn back in sales. Mojang is not interested in charity.

"There's no purely altruistic help-others spirit," says Markus, but quickly adds that he would like to invest in promising games. *Cobalt*, for example. *Cobalt* is a classic platform game that Mojang took under its wing shortly after the company was founded. Markus wants to do more of that. He'd rather Mojang act as a mother ship

The Mojang team at MineCon 2011 in Las Vegas, just before the opening ceremony. To the right, Markus's sister Anna Hemming. Photo by Elin Zetterstrand.

for game developers with great ideas but empty bank accounts than employ five hundred people.

Just before MineCon, Markus had decided to invite his family along, for the trip of their lives. Anna, Ritva, and Markus's father, Birger, would each receive a plane ticket to Las Vegas. It would be one of the few times since Anna and Markus were teenagers that the whole family would be in the same place at the same time. The siblings recall that Birger was withdrawn during the whole stay. Markus had pleaded with his father before the trip. He was welcome to come, Markus told him, but only as long as he stayed drug-free. "I love you," Markus said when he invited him. "But I can't talk to you when you're high."

When the fans left his son alone for a short while, Birger told him he was proud and happy about what Markus had accomplished. But Birger had come directly to Las Vegas from the countryside of Hälsingland, so he also admitted that it was alarming to be among so many people. Maybe it was hard for him to come to terms with the fact that everyone was there to see Markus. Birger saw how the fans swarmed around his son, the boy who hadn't been able to tear himself away from the Commodore 128 at home in Salem twenty years earlier. The Commodore 128 they'd both spent so much time together on before their relationship deteriorated.

MineCon ended with a giant party in classic Las Vegas style. Deadmau5 stood in the DJ booth. One of the world's most acclaimed house producers, he plays *Minecraft* himself when he isn't busy getting sold-out arenas full of people up and dancing. Great Britain's Prince Harry was seen in the vicinity, which got game bloggers wondering if even royalty had come to love the shy Swede's creation. At one point during the party, Anna turned to her brother.

"You did it, Markus. You really did it."

When the family woke up the next day, only one thing remained to be done. A long time ago, Markus made his sister a promise that someday he would get rich and celebrate it by taking the family on a helicopter ride. Markus lay exhausted in bed, but Anna, Ritva, and Birger went down to the hotel lobby and into a waiting car. Still tired from yesterday's festivities, they boarded the helicopter and flew out over the Grand Canyon.

Markus and Anna have thought a lot about what their father said and did during those days in Vegas. They both noticed that he was quiet and withdrawn, but thought it was just because he was overwhelmed. During the last few years, he'd lived far from both of his children and city life. Now he saw his son greeted like a rock star. Anna describes Birger as impressed by what he saw, but also as worn-out. The siblings knew that his most recent drug-free period had, like so many times before, ended in relapse. It would turn out to be his last.

Around a month later, they received word that Birger had committed suicide at home in his village in Hälsingland.

CHAPTER 16

BACK TO THE BOYS' ROOM

AFTER MINECON, MARKUS took a step back. He took a leave of absence until the end of the year and spent most of it at home playing video games. He felt run-down. He needed time to rest, to be with his wife, and reestablish contact with the friends he'd hardly had time to see during the past six months. But most of all, he needed time to think.

The months before the Las Vegas trip had been insanely

hectic. It was out of the question for anyone other than Markus to put the finishing touches on *Minecraft*, and Markus had worked more or less around the clock to get it ready in time. Interviews, meetings, and the other trappings of success consumed almost all his free time. It wasn't what he'd imagined a couple of years earlier.

To understand why *Minecraft* became such a success, you must remember how everything began. When Markus released the earliest version of his game, he considered it an experiment. He wanted to see if he could, on his own, finish a more ambitious project than those he'd worked on before. He wanted to test his ideas and maybe, if he was lucky, make enough money to finance the next game.

It was all about creating games for their own sake and creating new and different experiences. It was not a problem for him that it involved spending long nights in front of the computer with no company. Others often perceive Markus as shy, maybe even introverted—none of which is out of character for skilled programmers. Writing good code, not least for games, demands many long hours.

For those who've never programmed, the code may seem a means to an end. But impassioned developers often speak of their handiwork with great affection. It's fun for them, stimulating, and even peaceful to grapple with abstract problems, the solutions to which are found by placing commands in the right sequence. Being as introverted as Markus, at least during some period of life, may be a prerequisite for truly learning the art of programming. A programmer who doesn't enjoy sitting all night long in a dark room, eyes glued to the screen, will never become an expert, in the same way that the soccer player who has to force himself onto the pitch will never become a Zlatan Ibrahimović.

Neither is it a coincidence that *Minecraft* was created outside of the tight framework of the established computer-game industry. At Midasplayer, Markus's ideas were too odd, and the game he wanted to make had nothing to do with those that had already proven successful. At Avalanche, a programmer couldn't just drop into the director's office and suggest a new project. In fact, when we ask his old bosses, they admit without hesitation that *Minecraft* would never have become a reality inside the walls of their companies. The idea was too strange, too difficult to fit into their existing product catalog. Most of all, it was untried. They would never have dared.

Perhaps Markus's decision to leave his permanent job in the game industry is the most important aspect of this story. It was only when he resigned himself to the fact that no job with a salary would allow him the freedom to design the games he dreamed of that he was able to quit and create *Minecraft*. At home in his apartment, no one told him what to do. Of course, he was crazy to say no to a promising career at Midasplayer, but he was crazy in exactly the right way.

The weeks before MineCon in Las Vegas, the world was spinning so fast around Markus that he almost forgot about all of that. His daily life by then had very little in common with the life he dreamed of. He'd never had better circumstances for doing exactly as he pleased, but almost all his time was eaten up by the game he'd worked on virtually nonstop for three years. Great changes were in the works for *Minecraft*: a subscription model, for example, and better functions for user-generated content. These were ideas that had very little to do with Markus's original vision. They were afterthoughts, intended to lengthen the lifetime of a game he felt he was essentially finished with. With each passing day, the feeling grew that he was getting stuck in *Minecraft*.

So he decided to quit.

Shortly after MineCon, Markus informed the world that Jens Bergensten was taking over as lead developer for *Minecraft*. Now Jens would have the last word in all decisions while Markus promised to stay in the background. Many people raised their eyebrows when Markus gave his share of Mojang's profits, $3.5 million, to the employees in early 2012. The decision was sudden. One day, at the office, he gathered his T-shirted colleagues and told them that they were now wealthy men. The money was divided according to how long they had been employed, so Jens received a lesser fortune. But considering the fact that Markus had already made almost twenty times that much on *Minecraft*, his generosity feels more comprehensible.

Markus could at least put one thing behind him. In March 2012, the court case between ZeniMax and Mojang about who owned the right to the name *Scrolls*, was definitely over. A settlement gave the creators of *Minecraft* the right to call their next game *Scrolls* but not to trademark the title. In addition, Mojang was not allowed to make a sequel to *Scrolls* using the same name. The agreement is almost identical to the suggestion Markus and others on Mojang's board of directors had made to ZeniMax almost a year earlier, an offer that had been refused. When Carl received the invoice from his attorneys, he saw that the case had cost Mojang more than $200,000 in legal fees.

Work on *Scrolls* could continue, but *Scrolls* was Jakob's game. No matter how much Markus liked the game, he was not going to interfere in its development. He would have to begin something totally new.

It is no small thing to follow up the most talked-about game of the decade. The pressure on Markus can be compared to a musician who has released an award-winning hit album. Everyone is waiting for something new, and they all have ideas about what is most important. Some emphasize making money, others point to what would be most interesting artistically. Markus knew that the next game could never be as successful as *Minecraft*. Nothing could garner him as much money or as much attention. Nothing, except possibly an immediate sequel, milking more from the same recipe for success. And that's exactly what Markus had promised himself he'd never do.

There was only one reasonable way to go. Markus needed to do something really strange. A game so weird that no one could accuse him of selling out or of being a one-hit wonder.

At the time of writing, the first images from what Markus earlier simply called "the space game" had just surfaced on the Internet. It takes place on a spaceship and will contain programmable 16-bit computers. Markus has decided to call it *0X10c*—a title difficult to interpret, let alone pronounce, that refers to the year when the game takes place. It's yet another nightmare for marketers and yet another game that the bosses at a larger company would immediately have waved off as lunacy.

The first few days, Markus sat for hours, sunk deep in code. He lives in a significantly larger apartment now than he did when *Minecraft* was created. He is married and has more money in the bank than he can spend in the rest of his life. Otherwise, not much has changed. The old school desk that used to house his LEGO pieces followed in the move. His programming stints in front of the computer are just as long as they were in Sollentuna. *Minecraft* is history, but Markus has found his way back to what he loves.

With a smile, Elin tells us about the Markus she now sees every day at home. He spends most of his time coding. His eyes are shining again, she says. One day, he burst out of his home office. He was exhilarated.

"I've done it," he said, talking quickly, "I've sorted out that thing with the shadows."

PART TWO

CHAPTER 17

BACK AGAIN ON A DIFFERENT STAGE

NOVEMBER 2, 2013. It's early morning in Orlando, Florida. It's hot, humid, and thousands are streaming in through the open doors at the Orange County Convention Center, where the third annual MineCon is about to begin. Two years have passed since Markus Persson took to the stage in Las Vegas, pulled a lever, and released *Minecraft 1.0* into the world. A lot has changed since then. And things are about to change even more.

The Orange County Convention Center is one of the largest in the United States, perhaps in the world. It lies halfway between the airport and Disney World, wedged between the family motels and fast food restaurants lining International Drive south of downtown Orlando. It's not a particularly charming place, but it offers plenty of space. And with 7,500 people expected to show up over the next two days, space is precisely what Mojang needs the most.

Just inside the lobby, a sixteen-year-old kid in a T-shirt and baseball cap is pacing restlessly in front of the main entrance. Behind him, smoke seeps downward from roof-mounted fog machines, forming an artificial barrier of sorts that separates the MineCon exhibition space from the public lobby. Only ticket holders are allowed through.

The kid doesn't have a ticket. He's decided to spend the day here anyway, hoping to catch a glimpse of his idols. Maybe even an autograph or two.

"I heard Jeb was here yesterday. It would be so cool if he showed up today too," he tells us.

Jens "Jeb" Bergensten did indeed walk through the lobby yesterday. Even though the conference hadn't opened yet, he was swarmed by fans within minutes. Today the Mojang team—Markus, Jens, Lydia, Carl, and the others—have retreated backstage to prepare for the opening ceremony. It'll be the third time they appear on stage at MineCon together, and it'll be the last opening ceremony Mojang hosts as an independent company. But that is something the fans pouring in through the entrance are still blissfully unaware of.

Like previous years, tickets to MineCon sold out within seconds of being put on sale. We're told more than one hundred thousand people tried to get their hands on them. The lucky ones—thousands of them—are now jostling for space in the massive, hangar-like room where the opening ceremony is to take place.

There are people here from all over the world. Just as in Las Vegas, many are dressed up as characters from the game they are here to celebrate. Some carry square cardboard boxes over their heads painted to resemble Steve, a Creeper, or a Skeleton. Someone brushes past us dressed in a full-body zombie suit. Others have worked hard to top last year's best efforts—we can't help but stare as a black dragon with flapping, mechanical wings makes its way through the crowd. The homemade costumes are all very impressive, but many more attendees than in previous years have opted for ready-made Steve heads instead, bought from one of the thousands of stores worldwide that now carry a full range of *Minecraft* merchandise. Among them Wal-Mart, Barnes & Noble, and Amazon.com.

As the lights inside the theater dim and the music is

turned down, the murmur of the crowd changes into loud applause. A single, bright spotlight is pointed at the stage.

"Please welcome your host and guide for MineCon 2013," says the deep voice of the announcer. "Here's Lydia!"

A beaming Lydia Winters strides on to the stage. She has long since stopped using her nickname "Minecraftchick." Her pink hair is gone, replaced by a short blonde cut parted to one side. But her smile is just as wide, her posture just as confident as it was in Vegas.

"Welcome to Orlando and, more importantly, to MineCon!" she says and peeks toward the crowd in front of her.

"As far as the eye can see, there are Minecrafters everywhere," she continues. "This is absolutely incredible." The audience cheers in reply.

She's done this before, you can tell.

Two years have passed since we last saw Lydia Winters take the stage. Then, at the very first MineCon, there was an almost religious fervor in the air. The roar when Markus first appeared on stage, the thunderous applause when *Minecraft 1.0* was released to the world, the chance to shake hands with, say hello to, and have a picture taken with someone working at Mojang. There was a physicality to the enthusiasm, a shared feeling of being part of something new and promising. Perhaps even something important.

Many, ourselves included, were convinced that right there and then, the *Minecraft* phenomenon reached its peak. We were, to put it mildly, wrong. The story has been told countless times since. The strange little game that went from nothing to worldwide phenomenon in just a few short years. Its creator, whose wealth and fame never seemed to stop growing. *Minecraft* as a beacon for independent video game developers. *Minecraft* as a testament to the power of the Internet community and social media to spread word farther and wider than any well-paid marketing department or PR firm could ever imagine.

But, two years later, people keep playing. *Minecraft* is still topping sales charts worldwide. Videos from the game are still racking up millions of views on YouTube. Mojang is still booking hundreds of millions of dollars per year in sales. Nothing indicates that interest in the game is anywhere close to subsiding.

Shortly after MineCon in Vegas, Markus handed over development duties on *Minecraft* to Jens. And in some ways, "Jeb" is the real star of this year's MineCon. Fans flock around him wherever he goes. He does his best to accommodate them. In a way, he feels it's his duty. Time after time, he puts his squiggly signature on foam pickaxes, posters, T-shirts, mouse pads, coffee cups, and whatever else the fans hand him. He smiles and listens intently as yet another ten-year-old offers him suggestions on what animals, features, or minerals should be added to the game. They've paid for their tickets, after all. Many have travelled far to meet him, perhaps making a holiday of it together with their families. He is well aware that for a *Minecraft*-obsessed kid, a chat with Jeb at MineCon will be the year's indisputable high point.

But truth be told, part of him would have rather just stayed home. He's done this enough times to know that socializing simply isn't his thing. Sure, he appreciates the attention. But the hordes of fans lining up make him nervous. He finds the stress difficult to deal with. He was so exhausted after the first MineCon that he took a few days off work just to wind down. This year will be no different. Besides, the workload back home is crazy. He stayed late at the office most evenings leading up to MineCon. He knows there will be just as much to get done when he gets back.

Smiling as he puts his name on yet another foam pickaxe, Jeb makes a silent promise to himself. Once they're back in Stockholm, he'll work up the courage to ask Carl for that pay raise. The one he's been waiting on for almost two years now.

For others at Mojang, the situation is more or less the opposite. In previous years, MineCon meant round-the-clock work for all of them. It used to be that everyone had ideas but no one really knew how to make them happen. Managing a convention of five-thousand-plus attendees is no small feat. Mojang has spent the past two years learning how.

Carl Manneh looks well rested, laid-back, as he strolls across the exhibition floor dressed in jeans and a T-shirt. The first MineCon was absolute chaos, he tells us. An outpouring of positive energy and enthusiasm that sort of came together in the end just because it had to. This year, by comparison, has an air of cool, collected calm about it. Carl passes the oversized *Minecraft* blocks spread out through the room as decor, the massive Steve figure looming nearly thirty feet high in the center of the exhibition space, the merchandise tables, and the small booths for visiting indie developers. Everything is set up and organized with the professionalism befitting a billion-dollar corporation. Which is precisely what he's managing nowadays. In Vegas, Carl worked more or less round the clock to make sure things ran smoothly. This year, he doesn't have to lift a finger.

Markus makes only a few brief appearances. He's part of the jury for the costume contest, but takes a seat a bit to the side of the others on stage. He appears on the main stage only once, taking part in a Q&A with Owen Hill, recently hired as Mojang's "chief word officer," a position that, at any other company, would be referred to as "director of communications." The back-and-forth between them isn't what anyone would call a hard-hitting interview, more of a laid-back chat between two friends. Or more precisely: between a boss and his employee.

Jens may have become almost as important a figure-head in the *Minecraft* world as Markus, but when "Notch" himself takes to the stage, the room is packed. Thousands of people sit watching. All the seats are taken. Many are left rummaging for space along the sides of the room. If it weren't for the massive TV screens on each side of the stage, they wouldn't be able to catch a glimpse of the man.

Markus has changed too, and noticeably so. He's not wearing his fedora, for one. He's dressed in a bright, well-ironed shirt. He's thinner than he was a few years ago. But above all, his voice is different. He sounds calm and collected. He considers his words before speaking them. The bumbling man who wasn't sure what to do with his hands on stage is long gone. Now, Markus talks in front of thousands without the slightest hint of nervousness in his voice.

Markus and Owen discuss his day-to-day life, his favorite games, and his thoughts about where *Minecraft* is heading. After a few minutes, Owen opens it up to questions from the audience. One by one, attendees step up to the microphone.

"How did you come up with 'Notch'?"

"Is there any specific mod you'd consider adding to Minecraft?"

"Did you get a car yet?"

Many, especially Americans, seem fascinated by the fact that Markus neither drives nor owns a car. But back home in Stockholm there is nothing out of the ordinary about a grown man in his thirties without a driver's license.

Next, a twelve-year-old boy wearing a green-and-black Creeper hoodie steps up.

"How much money do you have?"

There's a ripple of laughter through the audience. Notch's wealth is as much a part of his legend as the game he created. Markus smiles, somewhat uncomfortably. He scratches his beard, seemingly considering whether to answer the question at all.

"I would say I'm being humble, but I actually don't know," he says, finally. "Because it's far more than I need, and there are some banking people who are taking care of it."

He waves his hand, as if to underscore how weird he considers these "banking people" to be.

"But it is quite a lot for a computer programmer."

Quite a lot? That's an understatement. At this point in time, Mojang has sold roughly thirty-three million copies of *Minecraft*. The original version for PC and Mac, created by Markus himself, now sits next to ports for mobile phones, Xbox 360, PlayStation 3, and, eventually, Xbox One and PlayStation 4. Markus's personal wealth now amounts to several hundred million dollars, and that's without considering his ownership share in Mojang.

Back home in Sweden, he is widely considered to be one of the wealthiest men in the country.

The shared enthusiasm of the thousands of kids attending MineCon this year is unmistakable. But the game they are celebrating, and the scene they are part of, has changed. The *Minecraft* community is no longer a niche subculture next to the giants of the gaming world. Because by now, *Minecraft* has outgrown most of them. Markus's game is no longer spoken of as a breathtakingly successful indie game. It's now simply one of the bestselling games of all time.

In December 2011, Markus announced to the world that he was stepping back from *Minecraft*. But behind the scenes, the news that Jens was to take over was already well known. The two had talked it through with their colleagues backstage at MineCon. By the time they waved goodbye to their fans on the final day of the conference, a clear plan of succession was firmly in place.

There were two reasons for delaying the announcement. One was to make sure *Minecraft 1.0* was out the door before news broke. Having Markus jump ship before then would have been embarrassing and possibly damaging. Two was an unexpected conflict that flared up on the way home from Vegas, and which couldn't be dealt with by anyone but Markus himself.

It all started, as so many things do with Notch, with a tweet.

"We also learned who not to work with at MineCon," he wrote just hours after the Las Vegas after-party, with superstar DJ deadmau5 behind the turntables, had wrapped up. "I'm very sorry for the behavior of the people we won't work with anymore. Celebrity or not, you don't f-bomb kids."

It was clear that someone in the *Minecraft* world, someone famous by the sound of it, had behaved in a way that Markus found unacceptable. But who? Would he tell?

Only minutes later, Markus added: "Yes, Yogscast."

For someone outside the *Minecraft* world, it is perhaps difficult to comprehend the bombshell Markus had just dropped on his fans. So imagine the repercussions if filmmaker Martin Scorsese, after *Raging Bull* had been nominated for eight Oscars in 1981, had suddenly announced to the world that Robert De Niro was a despicable person whom he would never work with again.

In its own microcosm, the equivalent had just happened. Simon and Lewis of the Yogscast were, at that point, by far the most well-known names in the still nascent community of *Minecraft* filmmakers on YouTube. Hundreds of thousands of viewers tuned in for their weekly broadcasts. Almost as many followed their every word on social media. At MineCon, the queues for their autographs had been only marginally shorter than those for Notch himself.

Markus went on to talk about how Simon and Lewis

had "repeatedly insulted people, talked behind their backs, refused to cooperate, and acted like total spoiled divas nonstop." They'd used "the F word" in front of kids, and they'd "demanded that we pay them to come here (nobody else got paid)." At least, that's what Markus now told roughly half a million people on Twitter. "They claim they're the reason *Minecraft* is big and that we should thank them more than anyone else in the community," he continued. "They're total dicks."

Within minutes, the Internet was brimming with speculation. Aside from the fact that onlookers now had a rare chance to watch as their idols traded insults in public, what unfolded looked set to turn into a power struggle of epic proportions.

It is indisputable that the Yogscast was a driving force behind the early success of *Minecraft*. Their videos helped spread word about the game and likely brought in thousands of new, paying customers to Mojang. But on its end, the Yogscast depended on *Minecraft* for the sizeable ad revenue generated by their films. Would these harsh words from Notch mean viewers—and advertisers—abandoning them in droves? Not at all, as it turns out.

Somewhat surprisingly, and without knowing what had actually been said at MineCon, many *Minecraft* fans decided to back the Yogscast in the ensuing conflict. Some claimed it was all a misunderstanding. That it was all a case of people missing the nuances of Simon and Lewis's brand of British humor. Others argued that it was irresponsible of Markus to publicly air his criticism before giving the Yogscast a chance to respond.

Simon and Lewis replied in writing a few days later:

"We are very disappointed by these tweets from someone we admire and respect. We can understand that it was the morning after the deadmau5 party and Notch was very tired, but we are still fairly upset. The quotes and actions that Notch attributed to us were not said by us or published anywhere by us. Therefore we are surprised and confused about where this stuff has come from—especially since the only time we spoke to Notch was at the interview."

In response, Markus backed down. It had all been a misunderstanding, Mojang now claimed. And besides, everyone had been a bit tired and grumpy coming home. What really happened behind the scenes remains a mystery—to this day neither the Yogscast nor anyone at Mojang will speak about precisely what was said. But as the conflict died down, one thing had become painfully clear. Markus was no longer the only superstar in the world he'd built. For some *Minecraft* fans, it wasn't a given to side with the creator of *Minecraft* when tempers ran high. Apparently, the Yogscast were just as much a part of the *Minecraft* phenomenon as Markus, even though they hadn't written a single line of code themselves.

Some surmised the conflict with the Yogscast was the real reason why Markus had stepped away from *Minecraft*. But the decision had been made long before those tweets were sent, and in many ways it marked a natural progression. Markus wouldn't trust anyone but Jens to get immersed in the code running *Minecraft*, and the pair had similar ideas on how to develop the game. Considering all the work that went into version 1.0, it made perfect sense for Markus to want to focus on something new. And he did: only days after handing the reins over to Jens, he sat down in front of his computer to get started on the game that would later be known as *0x10c*. It was to become Notch's first big project after *Minecraft*.

It's difficult to overstate how high expectations were. The man responsible for the biggest gaming success story in decades was starting to work on a new game from scratch! Every screengrab from *0x10c*, every tweet, every time Markus said anything to anyone about his new game, the games media went into overdrive. There was endless speculation, even though no one had actually played the game yet, and even though it still consisted of little more than a name and an idea in Markus's head.

"A sphere!" wrote a journalist at *PC Gamer* when Markus released a batch of screenshots, unable to contain his excitement over the simple fact that *0x10c* would not use the same blocky aesthetic as *Minecraft*. Markus himself described the game as his take on the spacefaring classic *Elite* from 1984, "except done right."

Another point of contention was how exactly to pronounce the title of the game. "Oxloc," someone suggested, as if the numbers were simply letters in disguise. Later, Markus explained that what he had in mind was "Ten to the C," with "C" referring to the speed of light. Mathematically, this translated to 281,474,976,710,656, which referred to the year in which the game supposedly took place.

What he imagined was, in some ways, very similar to *Minecraft*. The idea was a game, set in space, where the player would explore the universe in his or her custom-made spaceship. Like *Minecraft*, *0x10c* would take place in a world where almost everything could be interacted with. There would be no doors that wouldn't open, no computer terminals that couldn't be fiddled with. In fact, the computer systems aboard the spaceship were supposed to play an integral role in the game. The idea was that the player could write code for them, which would then affect how the ship behaved. The design of the terminals onboard—with light blue characters against a dark blue background—was clearly an homage to Commodore, the computer that Markus had started out with as a child.

A game of endless possibility, where the player could rework and rewire the world around them as they saw fit. Sure, there was plenty in *0x10c* that would be different. But the game was also a clear continuation of the themes that had been inherent in Markus's work from the beginning.

As time passed, expectations grew. Someone figured out how the virtual computers aboard the spaceship were intended to work, long before a playable version of the game was released. Enthusiastic fans immediately began writing software to run on them. Few game designers get such attention showered on their creations, even fewer on games that are still months or years away from release.

The situation now facing Markus wasn't very different from what might face a musician after a surprisingly successful debut album, after being showered with praise by critics and listeners alike. Sooner or later, the audience will start asking for more. You're expected to return to the studio and prove that the first time was more than just a fluke. Your creativity is tested in new ways. Some can handle the pressure and eventually release a second album. Others can't, and never do.

If making games was one part of Markus's life at this time, another newfound interest had come with his newfound fame and fortune: a string of lavish parties and extravagant holidays. That Markus had a taste for the luxurious was clear to anyone who had attended MineCon, at least those who took part in the over-the-top after-party, held at one of the most exclusive clubs in the city. It was soon followed by a series of even more outlandish events.

Markus made a habit out of hosting parties in conjunction with gaming conventions or developer gatherings. Anywhere he went, superstar DJs were flown in with him. Skrillex, deadmau5, Avicii, and Diplo, names usually associated with packed dance floors in Ibiza or Manhattan, all performed at events hosted by Markus. Sometimes, doors were open to the public and thousands joined in. At other times, Markus reserved invitations for fellow developers and industry people. His parties all bore the name ".party()," an inside joke for programmers. The name refers to a function in a programming language.

It's difficult to overstate the lavishness of Notch's roving party machine. The DJs performing charge hundreds of thousands of dollars for each performance. Markus didn't hesitate to refurbish whole buildings to ensure that the atmosphere was just right. In the summer of 2012, he hosted an after-party following the PAX gaming convention in Seattle. The WaMu Theater was reserved and redecorated to fit more than three thousand people. A custom-built stage and projection screens were erected, showing images of a fedora hat next to the ".party()" logo. Avicii—another Swedish export—was flown in to deejay. Pixelated red clouds hung from the ceiling as a reminder of the digital world that had paid for it all. Markus also had a special toy constructed for himself: a handheld remote with a single red button in the middle.

Whenever he pressed it, the fog machines mounted in the ceiling would erupt in a cloud of white smoke, slowly covering the dance floor.

A promotional film recorded at the party, made by the organizers Markus had hired, ends with a sequence in slow motion. With his back toward the camera, facing the dance floor, a man shakes a bottle of champagne up and down until the seal breaks. A fountain of sparkling white wine erupts over the cheering crowd in front of him.

In Paris, where MineCon 2012 was held, Markus took over the newly opened Cité du Cinéma studio complex, owned by filmmaker Luc Besson. He had fireplaces set up at the entrance, booked Skrillex as a DJ, and fenced in a three-thousand-square-foot VIP area for himself and his invited guests.

Markus's private life had changed too. During the summer of 2012, he and Elin decided to go their separate ways. Markus broke the news himself on Twitter, confirming that he was now single and ending with the hashtag #MixedEmotions.

Behind the scenes, his relationship with Jens had also turned sour. The unraveling had started just after the first MineCon in Vegas. Jens was of course grateful for the chance he'd been given to step up and take charge of *Minecraft*. But it also made him realize how valuable his contributions to the game would be. With his confidence boosted by the promotion, he worked up the courage to approach Markus and ask for a sizeable pay raise.

It didn't work out as he had planned. Jens clearly remembers how the heated argument that followed put a serious dent in their friendship. When Markus famously decided to distribute his 2011 dividends among the Mojang staff, Jens had been promised an extra bonus to follow. It came with the condition that he remain with the company for at least three more years. This, together with Jens asking for a higher salary, may have caused the rift between them. Jens felt like he was being held hostage by the three-year clause. Maybe Markus had interpreted his request for a raise as a threat that he would leave otherwise. Ever since, Jens has avoided talking to Markus about money.

With time, the pair drifted apart. They eventually stopped seeing each other outside of work altogether. Jens did show up at a few of Notch's parties, but mainly out of a sense of duty. He felt as if Markus only spoke to him about matters to do with work, which was the one area where they still saw eye to eye. In fact, he was finding it difficult to relate to the man who now seemed more concerned with lavish parties than with the games that had once brought them together.

With that said, the three-year clause did its job. Jens now admits that he was close to resigning from Mojang at several points. The main reason he stayed on board, he says, was the money he was due to receive when the three-year clause expired at the end of 2014.

All in all, Markus was slowly redefining his public persona. Before, he had been known as a shy, bumbling games developer, proudly ignorant of money, business, and pretty much everything except obscure video games. Now, he was increasingly talked about as the gaming world's most outrageous party animal, with a jet-setting lifestyle to match his bulging bank account.

This was one side of Markus's life during the year that followed *Minecraft 1.0*. Long hours of coding, alone in front of the screen, was another. It would soon be apparent which had the upper hand.

In the beginning, work on *0x10c* progressed smoothly. New screenshots were posted regularly, and in April Markus announced that the title he had in mind was legally in the clear (an obvious nod to the "Scrolls"-Bethesda debacle of previous years). Carl Manneh found it difficult to hide his enthusiasm for what was going on. A new game was being born at Mojang. A game designed and created by Notch himself, meaning millions of dollars of free publicity. "Markus is in a state of creative brilliance at the moment," he told a reporter from *Forbes* magazine, fanning the flames of hype and expectation. "I'm doing the best I can to block anyone who wants to interfere with that."

But a few short months later, things went quiet. As the new year approached, it became painfully clear that progress on the new game had slowed. Soon a year had passed since the announcement. *0x10c* was still nowhere near finished.

The delay had nothing to do with a vain pursuit of perfection. Just like with *Minecraft*, the plan was to release an early alpha build of *0x10c* to the public, as soon as Markus had something that even resembled a playable game on his hands. But what he'd come up with so far simply wasn't enough even for that. For a while, Markus even considered outsourcing some of the work to another developer, just to make progress. Clearly, something had to change if the game were ever to be finished. The signs of creative block were impossible to ignore.

In March 2013, Markus flew to San Francisco to attend the Game Developers Conference. In a hotel bar, he bumped into Brian Crecente, a well-known gaming journalist writing for Polygon.com. Crecente was having a chat with Mojang cofounder Jakob Porser, but as Markus sat down the conversation drifted toward him and his new game. Speaking to the reporter, he admitted that work on *0x10c* had ground to a halt. It was, to the outside world at least, surprising news.

"Are you definitely releasing it?" Crecente asked. "It depends," Markus answered, "if it's just going to be me and I'm going to still feel this kind of weird pressure, It's not really pressure, it's just some kind of weird creative block that's been going on for too long, and [0x10c] is going to be put on ice until we can fix that."

A few months later, in August, Markus had something of an epiphany. He'd taken a break from everything to compete in 7DFPS (short for Seven-Day First-Person Shooter). It was a competition for game developers, similar to the ones Markus had taken part in many times in the past. The aim was to create a first-person shooter in, as the name suggested, as little as seven days. Some competitions of the sort last for as little as twenty-four hours, but creating a first-person shooter is no small feat. Given the complexity of the genre, seven days was still absurdly little time. And indeed, the whole point of the competition was to encourage focus and see what results could be had from working under pressure.

Markus competed his work in time. The game he released was called *Shambles*, a fairly simple zombie-themed shooter described as an homage to id Software's seminal *Doom*. The results weren't bad given the time limit. But for Markus, *Shambles* turned out to be a game of enormous significance. Not the game itself, perhaps, but the process of designing it. Because for the first time in months, Markus had enjoyed his work. Coding was fun again.

Then and there, Markus made a decision. He would cancel *0x10c*. Instead, he would spend his time on smaller, more manageable projects. What he was looking for was essentially a return to where he had been when he started out, before *Minecraft* made it big and he became a celebrity. He took part in several more developer competitions. He released a slew of games that had taken him a day or two to put together. A few made headlines and attracted some attention on YouTube before being forgotten a few days later. Not because they were particularly noteworthy but because of who had made them. They had been designed by Notch after all—the creator of *Minecraft* had finally gotten round to creating something new.

As Markus struggled with his motivations as a designer, Mojang kept growing. By international standards it was still a small studio, as measured in number of employees, but it had long since outgrown the small apartment in Södermalm where everything had started a few year earlier. Instead, the company had acquired a six-thousand-square-foot office in a former tobacco factory in Zinkensdamm, about a ten-minute walk from its old offices in Stockholm.

Carl Manneh was put in charge of transforming it into an office befitting the new superstars of gaming—himself, Markus, Jakob, and their employees. It soon grew into a project where delusions of grandeur mingled with tongue-in-cheek self-parody. When Carl sat down with the architects, he imagined the fictive tenant Sir Mojang as the guiding star for the project. Sir Mojang was a middle-aged British gentleman with impeccable taste for the finer things in life. The result was an interior design that resembled a parody of an old-world gentlemen's club. "Masculine and exclusive, yet informal and homely," as the architectural assistant noted after one of their meetings.

Some of the interiors, such as the wax-coated conference table in mahogany, were flown in from the United Kingdom. Thick, checkered carpets covered the floors. A pinball machine, a pool table, and puffy sofas in brown leather completed the look. For the final touch, Mojang commissioned large oil paintings of its three founders that were framed and hung on the walls.

All the employees had their desks in the main, open room of the office. The only exception was Markus and Jakob, who had their desks in a glassed-in area along the inner wall of the office. It was essentially a separate room, separating the founders from their employees.

Markus spent most of the time at work inside his private office, with the door closed. Others at Mojang remember how he would show up in the morning and sit silently in front of his screen until lunchtime. He'd hired a personal assistant to take care of everyday things for him. At around noon, she would carry a bag of takeaway food to him, which he ate alone inside his glass cage. Usually, he only came outside to throw his leftovers in the communal bins. After that, he returned to his chair and closed the door behind him.

The months passed. Jens kept working on *Minecraft*, adding new features and squashing bugs. Markus kept working on his parties and sometimes released a game he'd been working on for fun. Things could have continued like that, perhaps to this day. But Mojang would soon be thrust back into the spotlight by yet another conflict with its fans. One that would create the most serious rift yet in the *Minecraft* world.

Markus Persson. Photo by Kristina Sahlén.

CHAPTER 18

LITERALLY WORSE THAN EA

JUST A SHORT walk away from the festivities at MineCon in Orlando, a group of people was sitting down for lunch together. In the room were a number of representatives from Mojang, although neither Jens nor Markus, Jakob, or Carl was there. The others at the table all came from the ecosystem of server owners that had sprung up around *Minecraft*. Some of them managed multiplayer *Minecraft* servers on which others could play with their friends. Others worked as builders, designing and constructing the impressive buildings that helped attract new players to their worlds. The one common denominator was that they all made money from *Minecraft*. In some cases, a lot of money.

The mood around the table was tense. Everyone knew a conflict was brewing.

Just as the *Let's Play* phenomenon had created a new breed of professional *Minecraft* video makers, a whole economy had been growing around the fact that anyone could host a *Minecraft* server for others to play on. At its simplest, people would offer access to multiplayer servers at a price, a hassle-free alternative for those who didn't have time to configure their own at home. Such servers consisted of "empty" game worlds, and the gameplay experience was no different from playing *Minecraft* on your own.

Others had taken their business in another direction. By enlisting some of the world's greatest *Minecraft* builders they had created fantastic worlds for others to explore. Many even offered games of their own, playable within *Minecraft*. Among the more popular were remakes of other video games: *Quake*, *Dota*, and *Team Fortress 2* have all been recreated on commercial *Minecraft* servers. Add to that countless other games, challenges, and obstacle courses to discover and attempt to master.

On the server belonging to Hypixel, a well-known *Minecraft* builder, was a paintball game, a vampire game, and one where players had to navigate a floor made of explosive TNT blocks. On the PlayMindcrack server, the games on offer had names such as *Dwarves vs. Zombies*, *Pajama Jam Time*, and *Revenge of the Cookie*. What they all had in common was that they used the fundamental gameplay mechanics of *Minecraft* to create new challenges and adventures for players.

Many argue that *Minecraft* should not be understood simply as "a game." Markus's creation can just as well be seen as a social network, or perhaps as a platform for collaboration and creativity. The many games, adventure maps, and challenges constructed within *Minecraft* are wonderful proof of this: players coming together to repurpose the game and to bring their own creative ideas to how it is played.

But just as million-dollar YouTubers like the Yogscast had built their businesses from humble beginnings, so too had the *Minecraft* server scene matured over time. A key development took place when entrepreneurial server owners figured out how to charge players for access to certain features. Some asked for a fee simply for logging on, others asked for money in exchange for certain benefits in the games they offered. A few dollars might buy you a better gun, better graphics, or additional features that others had to make do without. On some servers, players who paid a fee gained the ability to fly while those who did not remained firmly on the ground. On others, paying players had access to otherwise locked VIP areas. Some went so far as to offer their own virtual currencies that could be traded for various features and goods in-game. Bright, cheerful advertising would demonstrate the latest features and encourage players to spend more.

It was, for server owners at least, a brilliant business model. Since everything was still essentially *Minecraft*, most of the development work had been done already.

There was just one problem. Many of their customers didn't fully understand the distinction between *Minecraft* itself and the services offered by a server. Not least parents of *Minecraft*-obsessed kids. Many had handed over their credit cards so that their kids could buy their way onto a popular server, but few understood that the charges were to companies and individuals distinct from *Minecraft*. When things didn't work as promised—and given the millions of *Minecraft* players worldwide, this happened a lot—they naturally turned to Mojang for a refund. But the money in question hadn't gone to Mojang in the first place.

Some called or e-mailed the Stockholm office. Others turned directly to the person they saw as *Minecraft* personified: Markus.

Not surprisingly, these conversations often turned sour. Mojang had a difficult time explaining to distraught parents that whatever their kids had spent money on, it had nothing to do with them. Yes, it had all still happened within *Minecraft*. But not really, and not the part of it that Mojang was responsible for. It was, to say the least, a difficult point to argue.

During the summer of 2013, the pile of complaints had grown so large that Mojang found it difficult to ignore any longer. It was probably just a matter of time before more serious fraudsters realized that *Minecraft* was a prime target, the thinking went. As it was, it would have been a simple matter for someone to sell virtual goods that didn't exist, and Mojang would essentially have been powerless to stop it. But regardless of the legal situation, Mojang would be the ones blamed for the whole mess.

Perhaps one reason why Mojang was fairly slow to react was that rules were already in place, at least sort of, to deal with situations like these. As detailed in the end-user license agreement, or EULA for short (a term that would later become synonymous with disaster in the *Minecraft* world), Mojang did not permit the sale of in-game items in *Minecraft*. The only problem with the rules was that nobody had bothered to enforce them. For years, Mojang had simply looked the other way. There hadn't been any problems so far, they'd reasoned, so why make a fuss? It was a policy that rhymed well with the independent spirit on which the company was founded, and Markus's general hands-off approach toward what players did with his game. After all, user-generated content in the form of impressive builds and astronomically successful YouTube films were partly what the company's fortunes were built on. In addition, the conflict with the Yogscast had taught Markus and the others a hard-earned lesson: going against the wishes of the community was not a decision to take lightly.

Since Mojang hadn't really bothered with the issue, most server owners had taken for granted that whatever they did was de facto permitted. Sure, some may have read through the *Minecraft* EULA before setting up their services, but few took the words in it seriously. Ridiculously long-winded and obsessively detailed user agreements are the norm for computer software. For example, whoever agrees to the EULA for iTunes also agrees not to use the software to create nuclear or biological weapons. Usually, companies happily add whatever unlikely eventualities their lawyers can think of, to cover as many hypothetical bases as possible. Almost everyone clicks "I agree" without a second thought.

End-user license agreements are, in other words, pretty boring things. When Markus was first developing *Minecraft*, he'd handled that fact in his own way. The early versions of the EULA were written by him, addressing the player directly. The tone of voice was friendly and relaxed. In essence, it all boiled down to one simple rule: Don't steal what I've created. "In order to maintain control of the project, I need all game downloads to come from a single central source. I hope you understand,"

Markus wrote. "I'm not going to put up a huge EULA. I'm trying to be open and honest, and I hope people treat me the same way back."

But over time and as *Minecraft* grew, the wording in the user agreement changed. Markus's original headline, "Copyright Information," gave way to a more formal-sounding "Terms of Use." The "I" of the original text was changed to a "we," representing Mojang as a company rather than Markus as an individual. A section headlined "Privacy Policy" was added. Little by little, the laid-back, easy-to-follow, and personal tone of the original message disappeared. The text was soon many times longer than what Markus had originally written. Finally, "Terms of Use" was again replaced. This time, despite what had been said previously, by the phrase "End-User License Agreement," or EULA.

The final paragraph of the text carried a certain symbolic weight, as it brought up Markus's close contact with players during the early phases of *Minecraft*'s development. His constant interactions with the community and his ability to pick up on promising suggestions had been key ingredients in shaping the game. Markus's open, collaborative attitude was also, arguably, a driving force in fostering the friendly and welcoming attitude of the *Minecraft* community as a whole.

But now, in the EULA, it was all described as nothing more than a cold and calculating, some would say cynical, business transaction. "If you come to us with a suggestion for any one of our Games, that suggestion is made for free. This means we can use your suggestion in any way we want and we don't have to pay you for it."

Despite the increasingly formal words, Mojang was yet to lift a finger to make sure server owners followed the rules. As time progressed, what had started out as modest experiments turned into very profitable businesses. Several *Minecraft* server operations soon counted their revenues in hundreds of thousands of dollars. They managed game worlds that had taken countless hours to build and were backed by powerful and expensive hardware to handle the steady stream of new customers. In short: many people invested plenty of time, effort, and money into their server operations. They were not prepared to give everything up because Mojang suddenly had a change of heart.

A few months before MineCon 2013, Mojang let slip the first signals that things were about to change. There were rumors of impending adjustments to the EULA, and that the hands-off policy toward enforcing it would be made stricter. Some server owners were contacted officially, and panic started to spread. Was all their work about to be rendered worthless?

Besides, the timing was suspect. Mojang was about to launch its own hosting service, known as Minecraft Realms. From a business perspective, this was perhaps the most important update to the game since the beginning. For years, Carl Manneh had brought it up whenever someone pointed to the inherent weakness of the *Minecraft* business model—that users paid a one-time fee and were then given all future updates to the game without extra cost. Sooner or later the market would saturate, people argued. There would simply not be enough gamers left in the world to sustain Mojang's profits. Given *Minecraft*'s explosive growth, that point was likely to arrive sooner rather than later.

That is precisely why Realms was so important. The idea was pretty simple: gamers would pay a fixed monthly sum to Mojang in exchange for having their *Minecraft* world hosted on the company servers. It was a quick and easy way to get started with multiplayer *Minecraft*, and it meant that players themselves no longer had to keep their computers running day and night (or, for that matter, worry about losing everything when their systems crashed). Much like Gmail takes care of your e-mail and Facebook takes care of your holiday photos, the thinking went, Mojang would make sure your *Minecraft* world remained online for as long as you wanted it to.

In Carl Manneh's eyes, it was a clever way of sidestepping the biggest financial weakness of the company he was managing. Mojang wasn't in need of money, quite the opposite, but as CEO it was his responsibility to keep the financials as sound as possible.

Competing server owners saw the situation differently. To them, Minecraft Realms meant Mojang was offering a service that was largely the same as what they had been doing for years. Did this mean their own subscriber bases would dwindle at the same rate as Mojang's grew? And, more importantly, were the tougher rules for in-game transactions merely a way for Mojang to sabotage the competition?

Anyone who had followed *Minecraft's* development could easily dismiss this conspiracy theory. The server ecosystem had done wonders for the success of the game. The rich tapestry of worlds to explore and amazing builds to gawk at improved the gameplay experience exponentially. This was something that Carl, Markus, Jakob, and everyone else at Mojang was keenly aware of. But the way in-game payments were developing was worrying, to say the least. Not just because Markus didn't enjoy phone calls from angry parents, but because it went against the ideological foundations on which *Minecraft* had been built.

Some servers offered items for sale that made players stronger, for example more powerful swords or rare potions. This meant players who parted with real-world money had a different, arguably better, experience than others. The same approach was common in many other games, perhaps most famously one released by Markus's previous employer Midasplayer. Shortly after he'd left, the company had changed its name to King. It had also released a new title for the iPhone, which had quickly grown to become one of the most popular games of all time: *Candy Crush Saga*. Just like when Markus worked there, King released new games at a staggering rate. *Candy Crush Saga* was at its core a variation on tic-tac-toe and thus a clear evolution of tried and tested mechanics. The real genius was to be found in the business model. *Candy Crush* levels are deceptively simple to begin with. The difficulty is cranked up slowly to make sure players are hooked by the gameplay. Soon, it reaches a level where most are inevitably stuck. But there's an easy way out of the frustration: A click is all it takes to purchase an item—with real money of course—that will make the level just a bit easier.

Such games, of which *Candy Crush Saga* is just one of thousands, are usually referred to as "free-to-play," sometimes stylized as "free2play." They are free to download and, well, play. But after a while the inevitable reminders that you can spend a little money to enhance your experience make themselves known. Sometimes the player pays for new weapons. Other times for help in overcoming a seemingly insurmountable task. The free-to-play model has proven itself time and time again, especially on mobile platforms. Many if not most of the top-grossing games on the App Store belong to the category.

Markus hated it. He would never allow *Minecraft*

to go down the same route. Not for as long as he had anything to say about it, at least. The business logic underpinning free-to-play steered game design down the wrong path, he believed. It changed the focus of the developer, away from making interesting games that were as fun as possible to play, toward making them just annoying enough and just a little bit too difficult. Why? For the simple reason that no one would agree to in-game payments otherwise. The art, if you can call it that, was all about hooking players with simple, addictive gameplay and then slowly, almost unnoticeably, making progress as annoying and difficult as possible for those who didn't pay. It had to be done carefully— if it became too obvious that the developer was trying to push the player toward payment most people would lose interest. The most skillfully designed free-to-play games—like *Candy Crush Saga*—masterfully tread the balance between addiction and irritation.

Free-to-play was simply bad for games, Markus thought. It changed the game designer into a manipulative salesperson.

And still, this was precisely what was happening to *Minecraft* outside of Markus's control. The items, skills, and features sold on *Minecraft* servers represented a move toward exactly what he despised the most. *Minecraft* in itself had a famously simple business model—pay once, play forever. But that didn't amount to much as long as server owners could do as they pleased.

With this in mind, the tense atmosphere at the MineCon lunch table was no surprise. On one side were those who wanted to put an end to or at least severely limit in-game transactions on *Minecraft* servers. They saw it as a poison that was slowly corrupting the community from within. On the other side were those that regarded the server ecosystem as a cornerstone of the *Minecraft* culture. All the fantastic worlds that had been created, all the minigames and jaw-droppingly beautiful builds were what made the game so different and unique. Forcing in-game payments out of the ecosystem would likely mean that many of the most popular worlds would be closed down. Because what would be the point otherwise? Not even the most dedicated fan would be willing to put so much time and effort into something without getting some sort of compensation back.

It was easy to see that both sides had a point. Positions seemed irreconcilable, and as MineCon came to a close, the ticking time bomb of in-game payments remained an unsolved question. One that was about to blow up spectacularly.

It all started with a few throwaway tweets, as disgruntled players and server owners began to vent their worries over Mojang's intention to start cracking down on in-game payments.

"Apparently, Mojang is attempting to remove donations to servers to help their Realms profits," someone wrote.

"Good luck in your quest to alienate the majority of your player base," someone else chimed in.

From there, the discussion spread to various *Minecraft* forums, then to Reddit. Within a few days, it had become the talking point of the entire *Minecraft* world. Would Mojang suddenly start enforcing rules that would effectively rob a large part of the community of their livelihood?

Well, yes, sort of. But not really in the way people feared the most. By mid-June, Mojang posted a short explanatory note online, meant to straighten things out and answer all remaining questions. The text can be summarized in two points:

Yes, from now on the rules are in effect.

No, we will not destroy the server ecosystem. "Let's get one thing clear: we love it when Minecrafters host servers," as the letter stated.

The idea was to sidestep the issue through an exception. Already, as a way to deal with the fact that popular *Minecraft* YouTubers were making tons of money through advertising, Mojang had added a clause exempting gameplay videos from the rule. This move had, in fact, helped reinforce Markus's good-guy image in the gaming world. In spring 2013 he'd been invited to a meeting with YouTube. Its legal team had realized that the thousands upon thousands of *Minecraft*-themed videos available through the service existed in a legal gray area. Technically, they belonged at least in part to Markus and Mojang, given the fact that they'd be recorded in his game. This meant he had a legal right to claim a percentage of the ad money the films had brought in. Markus hesitated, but eventually turned the offer down. He told of it publicly and was applauded for his decision. Especially in contrast with game maker Nintendo, a company that had recently received a similar offer, said yes, and been vilified by gamers as a result.

It's difficult to estimate how much money Markus passed on by declining the offer. In all likelihood, it would have amounted to notable sums even for someone as wealthy as he was at the time. Of course, the cynical take is that it was all a well-planned publicity stunt, or that Markus simply saw greater value in the fact that YouTube was chock-full of films promoting his game. But even then, there is no doubting the respect he gained through his decision.

Now, the plan was for Mojang to attempt the same thing again. The new rules contained yet another exception, this time for in-game purchases of a "cosmetic nature." This meant only items that changed the visual appearance of the game, but not the gameplay mechanics, would be allowed for sale. In other words, charging for a new hat was perfectly fine. Charging for a better gun, or a potion that made your avatar quicker or stronger than others, was not. It was an attempt at compromise. Mojang hoped it would allow them to get away with enforcing the rules as intended, while simultaneously avoiding the wrath of the community. But was it enough to let Markus and the others off the hook? Not by a long shot, as it turned out.

A reputation for generosity, it turns out, is a double-edged sword. It builds expectations, some of which can be impossible to fulfill. Through a series of clearly unselfish moves, not to mention his status as the god-creator of *Minecraft* itself, Markus's fame had now risen to a point where fans expected nothing but absolute altruism from him at every turn. In all likelihood the situation would have been different had he simply acted like a businessman from the start, because no one expects anything but greed from a businessman. Instead, Markus was left to manage a community that seemed impossible to please. Every action he took that could in any way be interpreted as selfish was met with disdain from thousands of Minecrafters. And Mojang's announcement of the new rules for in-game payments unleashed a flood of abuse. "Complete idiocy," someone wrote. "TONS of loopholes," another pointed out. "Notch has failed us."

"I wouldn't want to be Notch tomorrow," said Stephen "Francis" Williams, a popular YouTube personality, in a cheerless update about the changes. "We're going to see a lot of people closed down. We're going to see a lot of people hurt. We're going to see a lot of people have their money evaporate."

It's difficult to overstate the magnitude of the rift that was now tearing through the *Minecraft* world. Sure, there had been controversies in the past. Many people still remembered the breakup between Notch and the Yogscast a few years earlier. But that, like most other fights over *Minecraft*, had been symbolic. It had been an argument about behavior, attitude, and choice of words. What happened now was different—it was about survival. About which servers would be allowed to remain active and which would not. Millions of dollars were at stake. Not to mention the thousands of players who regarded servers at risk as their homes, in-game payments or not.

And, perhaps most importantly, Mojang and Markus were blamed for it all. "Wow . . . I thought Mojang were chill people . . ." as one player wrote in one of the many discussion threads about what had happened.

At that point, something snapped inside of Markus. Two days after the new rules had been posted, he sat down to write a blog post about the ordeal. His words convey disappointment and sadness.

"Mojang does not exist to make as much money as possible for the owners. As the majority shareholder, I'd know," he wrote. It was an echo from years past, when *Minecraft* was just beginning to catch on and Markus, even before Mojang was founded, invited Carl Manneh aboard so that he would not have to manage the business himself.

Then, he went on to discuss the server community, and their methods for getting paid.

"Some of them even charge quite a lot. I don't even know how many e-mails we've gotten from parents, asking for their hundred dollars back their kid spent on an item pack on a server we have no control over. This was never allowed, but we didn't crack down on it because we're constantly incredibly swamped in other work."

Being blamed for essentially destroying the community around *Minecraft* was clearly hurtful to Markus. Someone went so far as to compare Mojang with Electronic Arts, the third-largest game publisher in the world and a common symbol for ruthless corporate greed in the gaming world: "A lot of people voiced their concerns. A few people got nasty. Someone said we're literally worse than EA." In fact, Markus argued, the new rules were more forgiving than they had been previously. "People are still asking me to change back to the old EULA. That makes me sad."

His post did little to calm things down. Three days

later, amidst constant abuse directed at him and Mojang, he made his frustration known to everyone.

"Anyone want to buy my share of Mojang so I can move on with my life? Getting hate for trying to do the right thing is not my gig," he wrote on Twitter.

The tweet was classic Notch. Emotional, impulsive, and not something to be taken seriously.

Shortly thereafter, Carl Manneh replied publicly on Twitter: "aaand I'm already getting approached by potential buyers."

"Good," Markus replied.

Then, things went quiet. Most people dismissed the exchange as no more than sarcastic banter between friends. In fact, the first step had just been taken toward a deal worth billions.

CHAPTER 19

EXIT

SEPTEMBER 9, 2014. Days were getting short-
er and nights were getting longer as fall descended on
Stockholm. For almost two weeks now, the country's
Wall Street Journal bureau had been in close contact with
editors in the United States, especially in San Francisco.
Hundreds of e-mails had been sent back and forth
since the first details of an unlikely story had emerged.
Microsoft was in talks to acquire Mojang.

What was surprising wasn't that someone was interested in acquiring Mojang. There had been numerous

bids in the past—most recently, according to well-placed sources in investment circles, an unnamed tech giant is said to have offered more than a billion dollars for the company. But this time, the deal looked set to go through. This meant all three owners—Markus, Carl, and Jakob—had agreed to the sale. The price tag was rumored at over two billion dollars. So far, only a handful of people outside the two companies knew of the deal.

The Wall Street Journal has four on-staff reporters in Stockholm. One of them is Sven Grundberg, who covers the rapidly expanding Scandinavian tech scene. He was more than familiar with Mojang—the company was now considered the crown jewel of the Stockholm tech ecosystem—but on this particular story he would share the byline with three others.

It didn't matter much that Stockholm time was approaching midnight. *The Wall Street Journal* has editorial teams spread out across the world, with New York, London, and Singapore as central hubs, working in shifts that overlap around the clock. As the pieces of the Mojang-Microsoft story were put together, it was early afternoon in San Francisco. Time was of the essence—there were talks that other newspapers were chasing the same rumors—and on a story of this magnitude everyone wanted to be first. Losing the scoop to *Bloomberg*, the *Financial Times*, or even *The New York Times* would have been an embarrassing defeat. This meant the editors at *The Wall Street Journal* had to make a decision. Neither Microsoft nor Mojang would comment on what the newspaper had gathered up. But their sources were good and the information deemed reliable. They would run with what they had.

Sven Grundberg had left the office hours ago. At one minute past eleven, his phone buzzed to notify him of a new e-mail. It was from a colleague at the paper.

"Pulling trigger soon."

Tuesday, July 29, 2014. Jens Bergensten had caught the train to work as usual. He'd sat down at his desk and resumed coding where he'd left off the day before. A special mood hangs in the air in Stockholm during high summer. Traditionally, July is the time of year when people leave the city for holiday—all employees in Sweden are guaranteed at least five weeks of paid leave—with normal life resuming in early August. July is when the Stockholm air is at its warmest. The sea has long since thawed and the water temperature reaches a point where a swim can be comfortable rather than just a painful test of endurance. Stockholm is too far south for the midnight sun, but nights only last for a few short hours during the summer months. In August they start to grow longer again, and the air becomes chillier, as an early reminder of the cold winter months ahead. Many people tend to look at August as the best time of year to start something new.

But for Jens, life ahead looked set to remain pleasantly familiar. While Markus had clearly changed in the years since the two had first met, Jens seemed largely unfazed by all the attention. Sure, he was now in charge of one of the most popular games in the world, played by millions of people on a daily basis. And yes, parts of the celebrity associated with Mojang spilled over to him. He was regularly invited to speak at conferences all over the world. Sometimes, people recognized him on the street and stopped him for a chat or an autograph. But his manners and his demeanor had remained the same. Jens is soft-spoken, thoughtful, and with a shrewd, subtle sense of humor that can take people a while to pick up on.

As the summer of 2014 came to a close, Jens took comfort in the fact that everything in his life was pretty much under control. Nothing much looked set to change in the coming year, which was just the way he liked it.

That feeling would soon evaporate. This was the day when Carl Manneh asked to have a word with him, walked Jens into a conference room, sat him down, and told him what the three founders had been planning for the past few weeks. Mojang was to be sold to Microsoft. It was the biggest bombshell anyone could have dropped on Jens Bergensten. At first, it felt unreal. He could hear what Carl was telling him but his brain was unable to process what it meant. In his mind, Mojang was the shining star of the independent games scene. The company he worked for was the company whose founder had said over and over that making money wasn't the point. Mojang made games because making games was fun, and they did it in their own way. Sure, the money was flooding in, but mainly as an excuse not to do the boring stuff, right? The kind of stuff that Jens very much associated with working for a company like Microsoft.

In the room with Carl, he couldn't do much but listen. He remembers how his brain, perhaps as a way of pushing the feelings aside, kept avoiding the big picture in favor of practical details. What would Microsoft think about his and Mojang's dependency on open source code? How would he go about introducing his counterpart there to the quirks in his programming style? He did, however, insist on speaking to Markus personally. He needed to hear for himself that his friend was serious about this, that it wasn't just some elaborate joke his bosses had decided to play on him.

Jens remembers the ensuing conversation with Markus, behind the closed door in his private glass cage of an office, as calm and composed. They talked about how the *Minecraft* community would react once the sale went public. Some would be angry, others would feel abandoned. Markus was well aware that he would be labeled a sellout, someone who'd abandoned his ideals in exchange for a big pile of cash. He told Jens he was thinking of taking a break from the Internet. Perhaps he could just disconnect completely for a while, his reasoning went, to escape the abuse that was sure to come his way once the news broke.

The impending sale meant there were suddenly plenty of tasks to keep Jens occupied at work. Carl had immediately assigned him duties that had to be dealt with before the deal could be finalized. He was put in touch with Microsoft to answer technical questions, and was asked to hand his code over for review. The latter is standard procedure whenever a software company is sold. It could be compared to having a mechanic examine a used car before handing it over to a new owner. Microsoft needed to make sure there weren't any unpleasant surprises hiding in the thousands upon thousands of lines of code that made *Minecraft* work. Things that had been stolen from elsewhere, for example. Or strange work-arounds that would make future development difficult or impossible. This meant running everything through a trusted third party, guaranteeing that none of Mojang's secrets would reach Microsoft before the contracts had been signed and the payments made.

Jens was also asked, sternly, to keep his mouth shut. For now, Carl, Markus, and Jakob had to make sure there were no leaks that could jeopardize the deal. For Jens, this would mean an excruciating time of sitting in the office among his colleagues and friends, all blissfully unaware of what he had just learned, but unable to tell them. He'd been trusted with an unpleasant secret, and he'd much rather have shared it with his friends than do as his bosses told him and keep quiet. Even so, he kept the news to himself. Jens assumed that Carl had told him first because he needed Jens to get started on code review right away. Otherwise, they'd probably not have told him either, he thought. Not until the very last moment.

In all likelihood, Microsoft was well aware of how difficult it would be to retain the trust and loyalty of Mojang's staff. Making sure people kept quiet was one thing. More importantly, both companies had to ensure that everyone didn't simply hand in their notice and leave the moment the deal went through. The solution was to deploy the one thing this deal had plenty of—money. Everyone at Mojang was made the same offer: whoever stayed on board for at least six months after the sale would be rewarded with two million Swedish crowns, approximately three hundred thousand dollars, after taxes. A small fortune was being tendered as a peace offering, in other words. But for some, saying yes was far from a given.

Money, like everything else, is relative. At the time, Jens was not alone in being dissatisfied with his paycheck from Mojang. In fact, a shared feeling had for some time been spreading amongst the staff that they were not really seeing their fair share of *Minecraft*'s astounding success. Sure, Mojang employees received more perks than most. The regular trips that were arranged for employees would have made most people jealous. In May 2013, for example, *Minecraft* passed two important milestones as sales of both the PC and mobile versions passed ten million. To celebrate, Markus took his whole staff, with partners, to Monaco. Arriving by private jet, they had spent a few days driving sports cars, riding helicopters, drinking champagne, and partying on luxury yachts, all at the company's expense.

And yet, some couldn't shake the feeling that their hard work mainly benefited Markus, Jakob, and Carl. The three founders were yet to make anyone else a shareholder in the company, not even those who had been with Mojang from the start. This meant that the massive profits generated by *Minecraft* still went straight into their pockets, even though Markus himself hadn't done any actual work on *Minecraft* for over two years now.

Everyone else had to do with a normal salary, plus whatever perks or bonuses Markus decided to throw their way when he felt generous.

At any other company this would have been perfectly normal. But Mojang was different, or at least it gave the impression of being different. The company projected an image of itself as a closely knit, easygoing group of friends. There were constant parties and nonstop fun, a culture of honesty and openness where nobody cared much about who was in charge. In the first few years this had, by all accounts, been true. But as the company had grown the atmosphere had changed, and Mojang's self-image was by now squarely at odds with the reality. The distance between staff and management had increased. Many no longer regarded Markus, Carl, and Jakob as their equals, as part of the team, but simply as management. Mojang had long since ceased to be anything but a workplace.

"Management has been really good at keeping wages down. Instead, we've been told that Mojang is a nice place to work, that we get free trips to the Game Developers Conference and that we all receive a Christmas bonus," one Mojang employee told us during summer 2014.

Even so, people stayed on. Almost without exception. For some, like Jens, the decision had to do with money. The bonus he'd been promised was set to pay out by the end of 2014. But there was also a perception that the company they worked for, a highly successful, highly respected games developer, would forever remain a fixture on the indie scene. Given the massive fortunes Mojang had amassed in just a few short years, and given the way its founders aggressively guarded Mojang's independence at every turn, the assumption was not far-fetched. In a rare interview with *Rolling Stone* magazine, published in May 2014, Markus had outlined a ten-year plan of sorts for the company he owned.

"Hopefully, we are going to keep making money at Mojang, but if we don't, that's fine," Markus had said. "We just have ten fun years, and then, the last year, we'd say to our employees, 'If we don't make any money this year, Mojang is going to be dead. So you might want to look for new jobs.'"

The story gives the impression of Markus essentially making the plan up as he went along. Even so, some of his employees put a lot of faith in those words. It sounded as if Markus was promising them a comfortable future, if only they would stick around.

Only three months later, that perceived promise was broken. Many reacted with shock as they were informed of the impending sale. What would happen to their jobs? What would happen to *Minecraft*? Would the office remain in Stockholm or was Microsoft intending to ship everything off to Seattle, where Mojang would become a minuscule part of the hundred-thousand-strong Microsoft workforce? There were many questions but few answers. And just to make matters worse, no one was allowed to say a word about what was about to happen.

News of the sale changed things at Mojang. Some felt betrayed by Markus's decision. Morale plummeted. "People felt like the world was coming to an end," one longtime Mojang employee told us shortly after the news broke. On Fridays, many began leaving work early. They'd walk over to Southside, an Irish pub a few blocks down the street, to share a few beers and try to process what was about to happen.

August gave way to September. As is always the case with big corporate acquisitions, time meant more parties learning about what was going to happen. A team at Mannheimer Swartling, a well-known Swedish law agency, was tasked by Mojang with sorting through the legal aspects of the sale. JPMorgan Chase & Co. provided financial advice for Carl, Markus, and Jakob in the United States. As the circle of trust widened, so did the risk of leaks. It was at around this time that information about the sale reached reporters at *The Wall Street Journal*.

As the story broke, many remained skeptical. Even people close to Mojang found it all too unlikely, too difficult to square with what Markus and Mojang had always stood for. Newspapers all over the world tried frantically to confirm the story with either Mojang or Microsoft, but both parties remained silent. Mojang was used to attention, but not like this. Games journalists, YouTubers, and bloggers would shower the company with attention whenever *Minecraft* was updated. Mainstream newspapers covering *Minecraft* would usually settle with recounting the tale of Markus's sudden and unexpected rise to fame and fortune. Now things were different. A reporter from *Bloomberg* parked himself outside the Mojang office in Stockholm and asked whoever entered to comment on the sale. They all declined, as they'd been told to do. Daniel Rosenfeld, better known by his stage name C418, the composer of the *Minecraft* soundtrack, was the first person associated with *Minecraft* to share his feelings about the sale. "The days before the sale went through, I felt betrayed by Markus," he told *The Guardian* in a fall 2014 interview, adding that since then he had gained a better understanding of Markus's motives. "Markus just wants to be left alone to make little games that no one cares about. That viewpoint makes sense to me," he said.

But at the time, what most people failed to notice was that everything had, in fact, played out in public already. According to sources familiar with the deal, Microsoft had approached Mojang as a direct response to Markus's tweet about selling his share of Mojang. This is what Carl was referring to when he replied. Markus's response—"good"—hadn't been a joke. It had been an open invitation to Microsoft to continue its advances.

Six days after the story broke, Mojang and Microsoft both confirmed the sale. The price tag was somewhat higher than what had been reported: 2.5 billion dollars. It was by far the biggest move yet for Microsoft's new CEO Satya Nadella, who had assumed his role only six months prior. In a press release, he praised *Minecraft* as something much larger, and with much more potential, than just another video game. "*Minecraft* is more than a great game franchise—it is an open world platform, driven by a vibrant community we care deeply about, and rich with new opportunities for that community and for Microsoft," he wrote.

What followed had a hint of desperation to it. Microsoft emphasized, over and over again, how well it intended to nurture *Minecraft* and the community around it: "the high level of creativity from the community will continue the game's success," said Carl Manneh in the Microsoft press release. He was followed by Microsoft's Xbox chief Phil Spencer: "We are going to maintain *Minecraft* and its community in all the ways people love today, with a commitment to nurture and grow it long into the future."

Clearly, Microsoft was well aware of the inevitable culture clash that would follow the acquisition. It is an open question whether statements such as these, devoid of emotion and expressed in dry, neutral corporate-speak, made matters better or worse.

But there was also another letter, written by Markus himself. It was a personal, heartfelt note, fundamentally at odds with the corporate world *Minecraft* was now to become part of. In it, the creator of *Minecraft* talks of selling his life's work, his fear of being seen as a traitor, and, most notably, his reasons for accepting Microsoft's offer.

"I've become a symbol," Markus wrote, without attaching any positive meaning to the word. "I don't want to be a symbol, responsible for something huge that I don't understand, that I don't want to work on, that keeps coming back to me."

"Something huge" meant pretty much everything the world outside associated with him. A hundred million players. Hundreds of millions of dollars in sales. Thousands upon thousands of fans, all voicing their strong opinions on everything and anything to do with *Minecraft*. And above all else, his own role as the man responsible for it all, the focal point and single most powerful individual in a community of millions. The founder of a company worth billions. "I'm not an entrepreneur. I'm not a CEO. I'm a nerdy computer programmer who likes to have opinions on Twitter."

The final sentences of his letter were quoted in newspapers all over the world. "It's not about the money. It's about my sanity."

The official communications mainly confirmed

what was already known. But one important new detail emerged: Markus, Jakob, and Carl would all leave Mojang as soon as the sale was done. None of them said anything about future plans and none promised any involvement in Mojang going forward.

In large, corporate acquisitions such as this one, reassurances are commonly given. This could mean that the founders are given seats on the board of the acquiring company, that they agree to stay on as "advisers," or perhaps simply that they offer to remain in charge during the transition into new ownership. The idea is to avoid too much of a sudden change. Familiar faces in management can go a long way toward avoiding a sudden collapse of a business, as too many things change around employees, customers, and partners at once. The enormous symbolic power of Markus and, to a lesser extent, Carl and Jakob, makes it even more noteworthy that there was no such agreement in place for Microsoft and Mojang. It's highly unlikely that Microsoft would have accepted Markus's immediate departure without making a fuss about it. Without knowing exactly what was said, the only reasonable explanation is that Markus had demanded from the start to be able to cut all ties to Mojang as soon as the deal was finalized.

Taken together with Markus's emotional statements about the sale, this fact paints a very different story from the one usually associated with billion-dollar tech start-up exits. One with little room for magnum-sized bottles of celebratory champagne or euphoric exit interviews with newly minted billionaires.

For Markus, handing control of his company to someone else seemed not to be an unfortunate side effect of the sale, but the whole point.

Mojang was created to realize a dream. Markus and Jakob had wanted to create a space of freedom and independence. A place where they could decide for themselves what to do and how, free from demanding bosses and a relentless, soul-destroying focus on profitability and sales. The money from *Minecraft* would be used to protect their boyhood dream from the world outside.

But with time, that dream had, more or less inadvertently, grown into an empire. One that symbolized something else entirely from what they originally intended. A community of millions, lucrative merchandise and licensing deals, and riches beyond what Markus, Jakob, and Carl could ever have imagined. All thanks to a game that, itself, hadn't changed significantly in its five-year lifespan. Mojang had outgrown its role as a small, rebellious challenger. It was now a stark reminder of the slow-moving corporate world that Markus, in the past, had refused to be part of.

Even if the whole point of the sale was to give Markus the catharsis he craved, others were surprised at how quickly he disappeared from the picture. When Microsoft sent a delegation for its first official visit to Mojang in Stockholm, Markus wasn't around. Few if any of his employees knew for sure, but it was rumored that he'd just returned from a few days in Vegas with Jakob. Either way, he was either too tired or too uninterested to show up in person. The task of representing Mojang to its new owners fell on Carl.

It was just past nine in the morning as Matt Booty, general manager at Microsoft Game Studios, made his entrance at the Mojang headquarters in Stockholm. He had brought a delegation of seven people with him, and made sure everyone was properly introduced before he began laying out his plans. Everyone who was present from Mojang listened intently, even though few new facts were presented.

Why had Microsoft bought Mojang? Simply because it was up for sale. What would happen to *Scrolls*? We'll see. Such a vague answer was less controversial than it may seem from the outside. As a matter of fact, the future of Jakob's collectible card game had been up for discussion many times in the past already. It had found a dedicated fanbase of a few thousand players. Not bad for an independently developed video game, but an abject failure next to *Minecraft*.

According to people present at the meeting, Matt Booty misspoke several times when discussing Mojang's future. Instead of saying Mojang he referred to the company simply as *Minecraft*, quickly correcting himself. For the others in the room, it was awkward to say the least. Less than half of them worked directly with *Minecraft*. Every time the man from Microsoft confused the name of the company he'd acquired with the game it was known for, he inadvertently pointed to the elephant in the room. Yes, Microsoft had acquired all of Mojang. But it was only really interested in *Minecraft*.

Even so, the same generous retainer was offered to everyone at Mojang. In addition, all employees were guaranteed their monthly wages for two full years, even if Microsoft shut down the Stockholm office and relocated *Minecraft* development to its headquarters in Redmond. At least one Mojang employee would go on to decline the offer.

It took several more weeks of formalities before ownership of Mojang could officially be handed over. When the papers were signed and the code properly reviewed and approved, a date was set. On November 6, 2014, Mojang would cease to exist as an independent company.

The day before, Markus had put in his last day at work. Several others were in the office as he stood up to leave. He hesitated, not sure how to say goodbye. So he decided not to. He made his way past the desks outside where his employees sat working, past the shelves stacked with awards and prizes. He took a left out the door, went down a small stairwell, and stepped out of the building. The cold November air stung his cheeks as the door closed behind him.

THIS BOOK WOULD not have been possible to write without the help of everyone who sat down with us for long, openhearted interviews. This story is based first and foremost upon the memories of Markus Persson, as well as on those of his family, friends, earlier employers, and coworkers, who have all taken time to speak with us. Thanks are in order to all of them.

When possible, descriptions and statements in this book have been validated by several people. Where nothing else is indicated in the text, quotes and information come from one of these interviews, conducted during 2011 and 2012.

CHAPTER 1. THREE, TWO, ONE . . .

The information about MineCon comes mostly from our trip to the conference in November 2011, supplemented with interviews of employees at Mojang and others who were there. The event is furthermore well documented on the Internet. Innumerable YouTube clips have helped us to document what we missed when we were on-site. Information about the total numbers of visitors and such comes mainly from Mojang's own documentation.

CHAPTER 2. FOR BEGINNERS

The examples of impressive constructions in *Minecraft* all come from publicly available pictures and film clips on the Internet. There are too many of them on the web to mention. A search on YouTube will turn up the constructions we mention and many more.

CHAPTER 3. "DO YOU WANT ME TO FEEL SORRY FOR YOU OR SOMETHING?"

The information about Markus Persson's childhood and youth comes mainly from interviews with Markus Persson, his family, and his coworkers. The documentary film *Klassliv* by Noomi Liljefors and Caroline Mörner, broadcast on Swedish television in 1998, tells of the high school class in Tumba where Markus Persson's sister, Anna Hemming, went. The film helped us to describe the apartment in Salem and Anna's teen years.

CHAPTER 4. GAMES WORTH BILLIONS

Numbers and statistics about the game industry come from the industry's organization, ESA (Entertainment Software Association) as well as from the companies referenced. Statistics on the music industry come from their organization, IFPI (International Federation of the Phonographic Industry). For more facts, we recommend the Swedish video game industry trade group, Dataspelsbranschen, and their superb reports.

Karl Magnus Troedsson, CEO at DICE, and Lars Markgren, CEO at Midasplayer, have both been interviewed about the game industry in general and their respective companies in particular.

CHAPTER 5. "THEY JUST DON'T GET IT"

Information about Markus Persson's and Jakob Porser's time at Midasplayer comes from interviews with them both and with people in their vicinity at the time. Rolf Jansson, Lars Markgren, and Markus's wife, Elin Zetterstrand, have all contributed with their own memories of that period.

CHAPTER 6. MACHO MEN WITH BIG GUNS

Erik Svedäng, Nicklas Nygren, Jonatan Söderström, and Jens Bergensten have all been interviewed about the Swedish indie games scene and No More Sweden. The book *The Ultimate History of Video Games,* by Steven

L. Kent, is a very thorough run-through of the early history of the games industry. Those who want to learn more about Swedish IT history are also encouraged to read our own nonfiction book, *Svenska Hackare*, published in Swedish by Norstedts förlag in 2011.

CHAPTER 7. "THIS IS WAY TOO MUCH FUN. I BUILT A BRIDGE."

Information about the sources of inspiration behind *Minecraft* comes from interviews with Markus Persson. Zachary Barth, the creator of *Infiniminer*, was interviewed about his view of the game's success. The early reactions to *Minecraft* were found in discussions on the TIGSource forum (forums.tigsource.com), where the first version of the game was released. Ritva Persson and Jakob Porser's memories from that time have also been of great assistance.

CHAPTER 8. THE HEDONIC HOT SPOT OF THE BRAIN

Quotes and information from Simone Kühn come partly from an interview with her and partly from her research report on video gamers and their brains. The report is titled, "The Neural Basis of Video Gaming" and is published on www.nature.com. In spite of the fact that it's an academic paper intended for researchers, it's also interesting reading for laymen.

The book *Trigger Happy* by Steven Poole is an excellent introduction for those who are looking for a deeper understanding of computer games, and it has been of great help to us. It is now available as a download, free of charge, on stevenpoole.net. There is an abundance of more academically oriented books on the subject, for example, *An Introduction to Game Studies* by Frans Mäyrä. Mihaly Csikszentmihalyi develops his theory of flow in, among others, the books *Finding Flow* and *Beyond Boredom and Anxiety.*

CHAPTER 9. "YES, YOU SHOULD BUY THIS GAME."

Numbers concerning sales of *Minecraft* come from Mojang's own data. Via https://minecraft.net, you can follow the number of sold copies of the game in real time. Markus Persson's visit to Valve in the United

States was re-created with the help of his own, Elin Zetterstrand's, and Jakob Porser's recollections.

CHAPTER 10. THE SQUID SITUATION

The visit to Ljunggrens Restaurant has been described to us in interviews with those who were there. Scenes from Mojang's office were recounted by, among others, Jens Bergensten, Carl Manneh, Jakob Porser, and Markus Persson. In addition, we've visited the space several times. During work on this book, Mojang began the move to a new office space in Zinkensdamm, Södermalm, Stockholm.

Johan Brenner, a partner at the venture capital company Creandum, has been of great help with statistics on investments in Nordic IT companies. Per Strömbäck, spokesperson for the organization Dataspelsbranschen, has contributed thoughts about the Swedish gaming industry. The statement that developers are the most common profession among Stockholmers comes from the report "Yrkesstrukturen i Sverige 2009," from Statistics Sweden.

Concerning Swedish development of broadband, see the report "Broadband Quality Study," from Cisco, published in 2010, and the report from Post-och telestyrelsen, "Bredbandskartläggning," from 2011.

CHAPTER 11. A DILEMMA CONCERNING HOUSE CATS

The film clip showing the Starship *Enterprise* built in *Minecraft*, is at the time of writing, still on YouTube. In addition, there are a number of sequels, where you can see how the spaceship takes form.

Information about the number of viewers of YouTube channels comes directly from www.YouTube.com and will probably have changed since the text was written. The same goes for how many times a certain film has been viewed, the number of tweets on Twitter, and so forth. Several contributions to the official blog *YouTube Trends* (YouTubetrends.blogspot.com) describe Google's own analysis of the phenomenon. Comparison of the popularity of search words on Google.com can easily be found via *Google Trends* (www.google.se/trends).

Alex Leavitt, SethBling, and David Pakman have all given interviews.

CHAPTER 12. TOO MANY FOR TWO PIZZAS

Interviews with Carl Manneh and Markus Persson have been the basis for re-creating the scenes from Game Developers Conference and E3. Lydia Winters was interviewed about her background, her view of Internet marketing, and the *Minecraft* phenomenon in general. Numbers concerning Mojang's turnover and profit margin have been retrieved from the company's yearly report.

CHAPTER 13. MORE THAN A GAME

Details of the founding of MinecraftEdu are based on interviews with Joel Levin, Santeri Koivisto, and their coworkers. Mojang has confirmed sales information regarding this special version of *Minecraft*. Mats Hultgren, at Svensk Byggtjänst, has elaborated on the ideas supporting the project in Fisksätra.

CHAPTER 14. BECOMING A LEGO

Jakob Porser's and Carl Manneh's memories are the basis for recreating the legal case between Mojang and ZeniMax. The episode was also covered extensively by the media, among others by the gaming website Kotaku. (kotaku.com). Rolf Jansson was interviewed concerning his view of the success of *Minecraft* and his relationship to Markus Persson today. Interviews with Jakob Porser, Carl Manneh, and Markus Persson have contributed to our discussion of Mojang's present and future challenges.

CHAPTER 15. "YOU DID IT, MARKUS. YOU REALLY DID IT."

The interview with James Green and Ken Klopp was done on-site in Las Vegas. Sudden Wealth Syndrome and the psychologists, Stephen Goldbart and Joan DiFuria, are described in a number of articles, most from the years around the turn of the millennium. For example, we recommend articles in *The Economist* and on www.sfgate.com. For more information about how lottery winners actually become happier, see for example the study *Money and Mental Wellbeing: A Longitudinal Study of Medium-Sized Lottery Wins,* from the University in Warwick, 2006 (www2.warwick.ac.uk).

CHAPTER 16. BACK TO THE BOYS' ROOM

Markus Persson's own thoughts about the future are the foundation for our discussion and for the scenes that are recounted in the chapter. Elin Zetterstrand has also been helpful by giving her view of life after *Minecraft*'s breakthrough.

CHAPTERS 17, 18, AND 19

Markus Persson declined to be interviewed for the second edition of this book. Descriptions of events leading up to the sale of Mojang are based on our own observations and interviews at MineCon 2011 and 2013, off-the-record interviews with Mojang staff and others in close proximity to the company, as well as news reports and official communications. Numerous blog posts and Twitter feeds belonging to Mojang employees have helped us with additional detail.

The story of Microsoft buying Mojang was first reported in *The Wall Street Journal* and followed by reports in *Bloomberg*, the *Financial Times*, and others. Descriptions of parties hosted by Markus and Mojang are based on information from event organizers Production Club and numerous unofficial video recordings. Descriptions of the Mojang office are based on our own observations and visits as well as information from architects BSK Arkitekter. Markus's views on free-to-play are detailed in numerous interviews, notably one with gaming website *Rock Paper Shotgun* headlined "Pay To Play: Notch On *Minecraft* And Monetization."

■ IN DECEMBER 2014, roughly a month after his final day at Mojang, Markus Persson made headlines by reportedly outbidding Beyoncé and Jay Z for a $70 million mega-mansion in Beverly Hills. Tim Schafer, John and Brenda Romero, and Selena Gomez were among the celebrities who attended his housewarming party.

In March 2015, he gave his first and so far only post-sale interview. Speaking to *Forbes* magazine, he told of his decision to sell Mojang: "The day we announced it, I was going to shut down my Twitter [account] because I wouldn't be able to deal with it, but people were surprisingly okay with it."

Markus has started a new games development company with Jakob Porser, named Rubberbrain. Projects deemed worthy of pursuing are yet to emerge, however. According to *Forbes*, Markus spends most of his days online, idly refreshing Twitter and Reddit. "It's like a day care for us—grown-up day care," Markus told *Forbes*.

Markus addressed the disappointment expressed by his former employees at Mojang with a single comment: "We spoiled them, and their reaction hurts me."

▪ In February 2015, news emerged that **Jakob Porser** had stepped in as a main sponsor for Luleå Hockey, the local ice hockey team of his hometown. "Everyone spends money on their passions. This happens to be mine," he said in a rare interview with local paper *NSD*.

▪ Carl Manneh has stayed out of the spotlight following the sale of Mojang to Microsoft. At the time of writing, he has not announced any new engagements.

▪ Jens Bergensten remains as lead developer for *Minecraft* at Mojang. He still lives and works in Stockholm.

▪ Tobias Möllstam was the first of the employees to leave Mojang following the sale to Microsoft. He now works for Hazelight, a new studio founded by Swedish game maker Josef Fares, creator of acclaimed adventure game *Brothers*.

▪ Lydia Winters is still working at the Mojang Stockholm office as director of fun.

In July 2015, Microsoft will host the fourth installment of MineCon in London. None of the Mojang founders are expected to attend.

BELOW IS A list of all the computer games that are mentioned in the book, giving title, platform, developer/publisher, and release year in chronological order.

Spacewar! (PDP-1), Steve Russell, 1962.
Pong (Arkad and others), Atari, 1972.
Pac-man (Arkad and others), Namco, 1980.
Donkey Kong (Arkad and others), Nintendo, 1981.
Bomberman (MSX, NES, and others), Hudson, 1983.
Tetris (C64/PC and others), Alexey Pajitnov, 1984.
Boulder Dash (C64 and others), First Star Software, 1984.
Duck Hunt (NES), Nintendo, 1984.
Tales of the Unknown: Volume 1: The Bard's Tale (C64/PC and others), Interplay/Electronic Arts, Ariolasoft, 1985.
Gauntlet (Arkad and others), Atari, 1985.
Super Mario Bros. (NEX), Nintendo, 1985.
Saboteur (C64 and others), Clive Townsend, Steve Ruddy/Durrell, 1985.
The Legend of Zelda (NES), Nintendo, 1986.
Final Fantasy (NES), Square, 1987.
Herzog Zwei (Megadrive), Technosoft, 1989.
Minesweeper (PC), Microsoft, 1990.
Nibbles (PC), Rick Raddatz/Microsoft, 1991.
Day of the Tentacle (PC/Mac), LucasArts, 1993.
Doom (PC and others), id Software, 1993.
Puzzle Bobble (Arkad/Neo Geo), Taito, 1994.
Full Throttle (PC/Mac), LucasArts, 1995.

Dungeon Keeper (PC/Mac), Bullfrog/Electronic Arts, 1997.

Half-Life (PC/PS2), Valve/Sierra, 1998.

Grim Fandango (PC), LucasArts, 1998.

Counter-Strike (PC/Xbox), Valve, 1999.

Quake 3 Arena (PC and others) id Software/Activision 1999

Mall Maniacs (PC), UDS/Addgames, 1999

RollerCoaster Tycoon (PC/Xbox), Chris Sawyer Productions/Hasbro, 1999.

Unreal Tournament (PC/PS2/Dreamcast), Epic Games, Digital Extremes/GT Interactive, 1999.

Europa Universalis (PC), Paradox, 2001.

Halo: Combat Evolved (Xbox and others), Bungie/Microsoft, 2001.

Max Payne (PC/PS2/Xbox), Remedy/Gathering of Developers and others, 2001.

Battlefield 1942 (PC/Mac), DICE/Electronic Arts and others, 2002.

Tom Clancy's Splinter Cell (PC/Mac/Xbox/Gamecube/PS2 and others), Ubisoft/Ubisoft and others, 2002.

Call of Duty (PC/Mac and others), Infinity Ward/Activision, 2003.

Far Cry (PC), Crytek/Ubisoft, 2004.

Half-Life 2 (PC/Mac/Xbox/Xbox 360/PS3), Valve, 2004.

World of Warcraft (PC/Mac), Blizzard, 2004.

Hearts of Iron (PC), Paradox, 2004.

Motherload (PC/mac), XGen Studios, 2004.

Chronicles of Riddick: Excape from Butchers Bay (PC/Xbox), Starbreeze/ Vivendi, 2004.

Psychonauts (PC/Xbox/PS2), Double Fine/Majesco, THQ, 2005.

Peter Jackson's King Kong (PS2/Gamecube/Xbox/Xbox 360/PC and others), Ubisoft, 2005.

Narbacular Drop (PC), Nuclear Monkey Software/DigiPen, 2005.

Knytt (PC), Nicklas Nygren, 2006.

Just Cause (PC/PS2/Xbox/Xbox 360), Avalanche/Eidos, 2006.

Gears of War (Xbox/PC), Epic Games/Microsoft, 2006.

Slaves of Armok: God of Blood Chapter II: Dwarf Fortress (PC/Mac/Linux), Tarn Adams/Bay 12 Games, 2006.

Tom Clancy's Ghost Recon Advanced Warfighter (PC and others), Grin/Ubisoft, 2006.

Wurm Online (PC/Mac/Linux), Code Club, 2006.

Team Fortress 2 (PC and others), Valve, 2007.

Knytt Stories (PC), Nicklas Nygren, 2007.

The Darkness (PS3/Xbox 360), Starbreeze/2Kgames, 2007.

Clean Asia! (PC), Jonatan Söderström, 2007.

Burn the Trash (PC), Jonatan Söderström, 2007.

Portal (PC/Mac/PS3/Xbox 360), Valve, 2007

Blueberry Garden (PC), Erik Svedäng, 2008.

Spore Origins (Ios and others), Tricky Software/Electronic Arts, 2008.

Shotgun Ninja (PC), Jonatan Söderström, 2008.

You Have to Knock the Penis (PC), Petri Purho & Erik Svedäng, 2008.

Stench Mechanics (PC and others), Cactus, 2008.

Harvest: Massive Encounter (PC/Mac), Oxeye, 2008.

Blast Passage (Web) Markus Persson, 2008.

Fat Princess (PS3/PSP), Titan Studios/Sony, 2009.

Battlefield Heroes (Web), DICE, Easy Studios/Electronic Arts, 2009.

Assassin's Creed II (PC/Mac/Xbox 360/PS3), Ubisoft, 2009

Angry Birds (iPhone, Android, and others), Rovio/Chillingo, 2009.

Bionic Commando (PC/PS3/Xbox 360), Grin/Capcom, 2009.

Infiniminer (PC), Zachary Barth, 2009.

Wanted: Weapons of Fate (PC/PS3/Xbox 360), Grin, 2009.

Planeto (Web), Planeto, 2009.

Farmville (Web), Zynga, 2009.

Shot Shot Shoot (iPad), Erik Svedäng, 2010.

Gran Turismo 5 (PS3), Polyphony Digital/Sony, 2010.

Alan Wake (Xbox 360/PC), Remedy/Microsoft and others, 2010.

StarCraft II: Wings of Liberty (PC/Mac), Blizzard Entertainment, 2010.

Just Cause 2 (PC/PS3/Xbox 360/ and others), Avalanche/Eidos, 2010.

Battlefield 3 (PC/Xbox 360/PS3), DICE/Electronic Arts, 2011.

At a Distance (PC/Mac), Distractionware, 2011.

Keyboard Drumset Fucking Werewolf (PC/Mac), Jonatan Söderström, 2011.

The Elder Scrolls 5: Skyrim (PC/PS3/Xbox 360), Bethesda, 2011.

Cobalt (PC), Oxeye/Mojang, 2011.

AirMech (PC), Carbon Games, 2012.

Closure (PC/Mac/PS3), Eyebrow Interactive, 2012.

MANY THANKS TO everyone who graciously gave us the time to be interviewed, helping us piece this story together. Without you, this book would never have happened. Thanks also to Stefan Skog at Norstedts, for endless patience and enthusiasm; John Hagström, for brutal but well-meaning honesty; Dan Simon and Jesse Lichtenstein at Seven Stories; Jennifer Hawkins for her translation; Thomas Arnroth, for insightful comments; Mikael Hall, for office space; and to Deniz Kaya and Anna Silberstein, because you haven't left us yet.

TRANSLATOR'S THANKS

THE TRANSLATOR WOULD like to thank eleven-year-old Nicklas Lumiere for initiating her personally into the world of *Minecraft*. It was an enlightening journey. Kim MacKay was indispensible as reader and giver of great advice.

DANIEL GOLDBERG AND LINUS LARSSON are two of Sweden's best-known writers on new technology and the Internet. Their first book, *Svenska Hackare*, a nonfiction account of the Scandinavian hacker scene and phenomena such as The Pirate Bay, was published in spring 2011 to critical acclaim in Sweden. This is their first book to appear in English.